50 Holiday Feast Recipes for Home

By: Kelly Johnson

Table of Contents

- Smoked Brisket
- Smoked Pulled Pork
- Smoked Ribs
- Smoked Chicken Wings
- Smoked Salmon
- Smoked Turkey Breast
- Smoked Pork Shoulder
- Smoked Beef Short Ribs
- Smoked Sausages
- Smoked Meatloaf
- Smoked Stuffed Peppers
- Smoked Meatballs
- Smoked Pork Belly
- Smoked Duck Breast
- Smoked Beef Jerky
- Smoked Pork Chops
- Smoked Shrimp
- Smoked Mac and Cheese
- Smoked Corn on the Cob
- Smoked Meat Pizza
- Smoked Stuffed Mushrooms
- Smoked Lamb Ribs
- Smoked Tofu
- Smoked Sweet Potatoes
- Smoked Cheese
- Smoked Pork Tenderloin
- Smoked Chicken Thighs
- Smoked Bratwurst
- Smoked Cauliflower Steaks
- Smoked Ratatouille
- Smoked Meat Tacos
- Smoked Beef Burgers
- Smoked Lobster Tails
- Smoked Meatballs in BBQ Sauce
- Smoked Turkey Legs

- Smoked Chili
- Smoked Garlic Butter Shrimp
- Smoked Asparagus
- Smoked Beef Kabobs
- Smoked Beef Brisket Chili
- Smoked Stuffed Pork Loin
- Smoked Buffalo Wings
- Smoked Cornbread
- Smoked Crab Legs
- Smoked Meat Pies
- Smoked Eggplant Dip
- Smoked Beef Wellington
- Smoked Ham
- Smoked Pastrami
- Smoked Vegetable Skewers

Smoked Brisket

Ingredients:

- 1 whole beef brisket, about 10-12 pounds
- Salt (kosher or sea salt) and freshly ground black pepper
- Beef brisket rub (optional, see recipe below)
- Wood chips or chunks for smoking (hickory, oak, mesquite, or pecan)

Beef Brisket Rub:

- 2 tablespoons kosher salt
- 2 tablespoons freshly ground black pepper
- 2 tablespoons paprika
- 1 tablespoon garlic powder
- 1 tablespoon onion powder
- 1 tablespoon brown sugar
- 1 teaspoon cayenne pepper (adjust to taste)

Instructions:

1. Prepare the Brisket:
    - Trim any excess fat from the brisket, leaving a thin layer of fat on one side to keep the meat moist during smoking.
    - Pat the brisket dry with paper towels.
2. Season the Brisket:
    - Season the brisket generously with salt and freshly ground black pepper. If using a beef brisket rub, apply the rub evenly over the entire surface of the brisket. Press the seasoning into the meat.
3. Prepare the Smoker:
    - Preheat your smoker to a temperature of 225-250°F (107-121°C). Use wood chips or chunks (soaked in water for at least 30 minutes) to generate smoke.
4. Smoke the Brisket:
    - Place the seasoned brisket on the smoker grate with the fat side up.
    - Close the smoker and maintain a consistent temperature throughout the smoking process.
    - Smoke the brisket for about 1.5 to 2 hours per pound of meat, or until the internal temperature reaches around 195-205°F (90-96°C) for optimal

tenderness. This can take anywhere from 10-16 hours depending on the size of your brisket.
5. Rest the Brisket:
   - Once the brisket reaches the desired internal temperature, carefully remove it from the smoker and wrap it tightly in butcher paper or aluminum foil.
   - Allow the brisket to rest for at least 1-2 hours. This resting period allows the juices to redistribute throughout the meat, resulting in a more tender and flavorful brisket.
6. Slice and Serve:
   - Unwrap the brisket and slice it against the grain into thin slices using a sharp knife.
   - Serve the smoked brisket slices on a platter and enjoy with your favorite barbecue sauce, pickles, and sides like coleslaw, potato salad, or baked beans.

Smoked brisket is a labor of love that requires patience and attention, but the result is incredibly rewarding. Whether you're a seasoned pitmaster or trying smoking for the first time, smoked brisket is sure to impress your family and friends!

Smoked Pulled Pork

Ingredients:

- 1 pork shoulder (also known as pork butt or Boston butt), about 7-8 pounds
- Pork rub (see recipe below)
- Wood chips or chunks for smoking (hickory, apple, cherry, or pecan)

Pork Rub:

- 2 tablespoons brown sugar
- 2 tablespoons paprika
- 1 tablespoon garlic powder
- 1 tablespoon onion powder
- 1 tablespoon kosher salt
- 1 tablespoon black pepper
- 1 teaspoon cayenne pepper (adjust to taste)

For Serving:

- Barbecue sauce (optional)
- Sandwich buns or tortillas
- Coleslaw (optional)

Instructions:

1. Prepare the Pork Shoulder:
    - Trim any excess fat from the pork shoulder, leaving a thin layer of fat on top to keep the meat moist during smoking.
    - Pat the pork shoulder dry with paper towels.
2. Apply the Pork Rub:
    - In a small bowl, mix together all the ingredients for the pork rub.
    - Rub the pork rub mixture all over the surface of the pork shoulder, making sure to coat it evenly. Press the rub into the meat.
3. Prepare the Smoker:
    - Preheat your smoker to a temperature of 225-250°F (107-121°C). Use wood chips or chunks (soaked in water for at least 30 minutes) to generate smoke.
4. Smoke the Pork Shoulder:

- Place the seasoned pork shoulder on the smoker grate, fat side up.
- Close the smoker and maintain a consistent temperature throughout the smoking process.
- Smoke the pork shoulder for approximately 1.5 to 2 hours per pound of meat, or until the internal temperature reaches around 195-205°F (90-96°C) and the meat is tender and easily shreddable.

5. Rest the Pork Shoulder:
    - Once the pork shoulder reaches the desired internal temperature, carefully remove it from the smoker and wrap it tightly in butcher paper or aluminum foil.
    - Allow the pork shoulder to rest for at least 1-2 hours. This resting period allows the juices to redistribute throughout the meat.
6. Pull and Serve:
    - Unwrap the rested pork shoulder and use two forks to shred the meat into pulled pork.
    - Serve the smoked pulled pork on sandwich buns or tortillas, topped with barbecue sauce if desired.
    - Optional: Serve with coleslaw on top for added crunch and freshness.

Smoked pulled pork is a crowd-pleaser and perfect for gatherings or backyard barbecues. The low and slow smoking process results in tender, flavorful meat that's sure to be a hit! Adjust the seasoning and smoking time according to your preferences and enjoy this classic barbecue dish.

Smoked Ribs

Ingredients:

- 2 racks of pork baby back ribs (about 2-3 pounds each)
- Dry rub (see recipe below)
- Barbecue sauce (optional, for serving)

Dry Rub:

- 2 tablespoons brown sugar
- 2 tablespoons paprika
- 1 tablespoon garlic powder
- 1 tablespoon onion powder
- 1 tablespoon kosher salt
- 1 tablespoon black pepper
- 1 teaspoon cayenne pepper (adjust to taste)

Instructions:

1. Prepare the Ribs:
   - Remove the membrane from the back of the ribs. Use a small knife to loosen the membrane at one end, then grab it with a paper towel and pull it off in one piece.
2. Apply the Dry Rub:
   - In a small bowl, mix together all the ingredients for the dry rub.
   - Rub the dry rub mixture all over both sides of the ribs, coating them evenly. Press the rub into the meat.
3. Prepare the Smoker:
   - Preheat your smoker to a temperature of 225-250°F (107-121°C). Use wood chips or chunks (such as hickory, apple, cherry, or oak) to generate smoke.
4. Smoke the Ribs:
   - Place the seasoned ribs on the smoker grate, meat side up.
   - Close the smoker and maintain a consistent temperature throughout the smoking process.
   - Smoke the ribs for approximately 3-4 hours, or until the meat is tender and pulls away from the bones. The internal temperature of the ribs should reach around 190-203°F (88-95°C).
5. Optional: Wrap the Ribs (Texas Crutch):

- If you prefer extra-tender ribs, you can wrap them in foil (known as the Texas crutch) after the first 2-3 hours of smoking. This helps retain moisture and speeds up the cooking process.
6. Rest and Serve:
    - Once the ribs are done, carefully remove them from the smoker and let them rest for 10-15 minutes.
    - Slice the ribs between the bones to separate them into individual servings.
    - Serve the smoked ribs with barbecue sauce on the side for dipping, if desired.

Smoked ribs are best enjoyed hot off the smoker, with a side of coleslaw, cornbread, or baked beans. The combination of smoky flavor and tender meat makes these smoked ribs a favorite for barbecue enthusiasts. Adjust the seasoning and smoking time based on your preferences, and enjoy this delicious barbecue dish!

Smoked Chicken Wings

Ingredients:

- 2-3 pounds of chicken wings
- Olive oil
- Chicken wing dry rub (see recipe below)
- Barbecue sauce (optional, for serving)

Chicken Wing Dry Rub:

- 2 tablespoons brown sugar
- 1 tablespoon paprika
- 1 teaspoon garlic powder
- 1 teaspoon onion powder
- 1 teaspoon chili powder
- 1 teaspoon kosher salt
- 1/2 teaspoon black pepper
- 1/2 teaspoon cayenne pepper (adjust to taste)

Instructions:

1. Prepare the Chicken Wings:
   - Rinse the chicken wings under cold water and pat them dry with paper towels.
   - Place the wings in a large bowl and drizzle with olive oil, tossing to coat evenly.
2. Apply the Dry Rub:
   - In a small bowl, mix together all the ingredients for the chicken wing dry rub.
   - Sprinkle the dry rub over the chicken wings, tossing to coat them thoroughly with the seasoning.
3. Prepare the Smoker:
   - Preheat your smoker to a temperature of 225-250°F (107-121°C). Use wood chips or chunks (such as hickory, apple, cherry, or maple) to generate smoke.
4. Smoke the Chicken Wings:
   - Arrange the seasoned chicken wings on the smoker grate, leaving space between each wing for even smoking.

- Close the smoker and maintain a consistent temperature throughout the smoking process.
- Smoke the chicken wings for approximately 1.5 to 2 hours, or until they reach an internal temperature of 165°F (74°C) and the skin is crispy and golden brown.

5. Optional: Finish with Barbecue Sauce:
    - If desired, brush the smoked chicken wings with barbecue sauce during the last 10-15 minutes of smoking to glaze them and add extra flavor.
6. Rest and Serve:
    - Once the smoked chicken wings are done, carefully remove them from the smoker and let them rest for a few minutes.
    - Serve the smoked chicken wings hot with additional barbecue sauce on the side for dipping.

Smoked chicken wings are best enjoyed fresh off the smoker, with your favorite dipping sauce or alongside coleslaw, potato salad, or other barbecue sides. The smoky flavor and tender texture of these wings will be a hit at any gathering! Adjust the seasoning and smoking time based on your preferences, and enjoy this delicious smoked chicken wing recipe.

Smoked Salmon

Ingredients:

- 1 pound of salmon fillet (skin-on or skinless)
- 1/4 cup kosher salt
- 1/4 cup brown sugar
- 1 tablespoon freshly ground black pepper
- 1 tablespoon lemon zest (optional)
- Wood chips or chunks for smoking (alder, oak, apple, or maple)

Instructions:

1. Prepare the Salmon:
    - Rinse the salmon fillet under cold water and pat it dry with paper towels.
    - Check for any pin bones in the salmon and remove them using tweezers.
2. Prepare the Brine:
    - In a bowl, mix together the kosher salt, brown sugar, black pepper, and lemon zest (if using) to make the brine.
    - Spread a layer of the brine mixture in a shallow dish.
3. Brine the Salmon:
    - Place the salmon fillet, skin-side down, on top of the brine mixture in the dish.
    - Coat the flesh side of the salmon with the remaining brine mixture.
    - Cover the dish with plastic wrap and refrigerate for 4-6 hours to allow the salmon to brine and absorb the flavors.
4. Rinse and Air-Dry:
    - After brining, remove the salmon from the dish and rinse it thoroughly under cold water to remove excess salt.
    - Pat the salmon dry with paper towels and place it on a wire rack.
    - Let the salmon air-dry in the refrigerator for 1-2 hours until a shiny pellicle (a thin, tacky layer) forms on the surface of the fish. This step helps the smoke adhere to the salmon.
5. Prepare the Smoker:
    - Preheat your smoker to a temperature of 180-200°F (82-93°C). Use wood chips or chunks (such as alder, oak, apple, or maple) to generate smoke.
6. Smoke the Salmon:
    - Place the salmon fillet on the smoker grate, skin-side down.
    - Close the smoker and maintain a consistent temperature throughout the smoking process.

- Smoke the salmon for approximately 1.5 to 2 hours, or until the internal temperature reaches 145°F (63°C) and the fish is opaque and flaky.
7. Cool and Serve:
    - Once the smoked salmon is done, carefully remove it from the smoker and let it cool slightly.
    - Slice the smoked salmon into thin strips or flakes.
    - Serve the smoked salmon on a platter as an appetizer, or use it in sandwiches, salads, pasta dishes, or as a topping for bagels with cream cheese.

Enjoy this homemade smoked salmon with its rich, smoky flavor and tender texture. Store any leftover smoked salmon in the refrigerator for up to a week or freeze it for longer storage. Adjust the smoking time based on the thickness of the salmon fillet and your desired level of smokiness.

Smoked Turkey Breast

Ingredients:

- 1 whole bone-in turkey breast (about 4-6 pounds)
- Olive oil or melted butter
- Salt and pepper, to taste
- Wood chips or chunks for smoking (hickory, apple, cherry, or maple)

Instructions:

1. Prepare the Turkey Breast:
    - Remove the turkey breast from its packaging. Pat it dry with paper towels.
    - Rub the turkey breast with olive oil or melted butter. This helps the seasonings stick and keeps the meat moist during smoking.
    - Season the turkey breast generously with salt and pepper, covering all sides.
2. Prepare the Smoker:
    - Preheat your smoker to a temperature of 225-250°F (107-121°C).
    - Add wood chips or chunks (such as hickory, apple, cherry, or maple) to the smoker box or tray. These will provide the smoky flavor.
3. Smoke the Turkey Breast:
    - Place the seasoned turkey breast directly on the smoker grate, with the skin side up.
    - Close the smoker lid and let the turkey breast smoke at a consistent temperature for about 30 minutes per pound, or until the internal temperature reaches 165°F (74°C) when measured with a meat thermometer inserted into the thickest part of the breast.
    - You can baste the turkey breast with additional olive oil or butter during smoking to keep it moist.
4. Rest and Serve:
    - Once the smoked turkey breast reaches the desired temperature, carefully remove it from the smoker.
    - Let the turkey breast rest for about 10-15 minutes before slicing. This allows the juices to redistribute within the meat.
    - Slice the smoked turkey breast against the grain into thin slices.
5. Enjoy:
    - Serve the smoked turkey breast as a main course with your favorite sides, such as mashed potatoes, stuffing, or roasted vegetables.

- Alternatively, use the smoked turkey breast in sandwiches, wraps, salads, or pasta dishes.

Tips:

- Use a meat thermometer to ensure the turkey breast is cooked to a safe internal temperature of 165°F (74°C).
- Experiment with different wood chips or chunks to customize the flavor of your smoked turkey breast.
- Feel free to add your favorite herbs or spices to the turkey breast before smoking for additional flavor.

This smoked turkey breast recipe is simple yet incredibly flavorful. It's perfect for any occasion and is sure to impress your family and friends with its delicious smoky taste! Adjust the smoking time based on the size of your turkey breast and your smoker's temperature for best results.

Smoked Pork Shoulder

Ingredients:

- 1 pork shoulder (also known as pork butt), bone-in or boneless, about 8-10 pounds
- Yellow mustard (optional, for binding)
- Pork dry rub (see recipe below)
- Wood chips or chunks for smoking (hickory, apple, cherry, or pecan)

Pork Dry Rub:

- 1/4 cup brown sugar
- 2 tablespoons paprika
- 2 tablespoons kosher salt
- 1 tablespoon garlic powder
- 1 tablespoon onion powder
- 1 tablespoon black pepper
- 1 tablespoon chili powder
- 1 teaspoon cayenne pepper (adjust to taste)

Instructions:

1. Prepare the Pork Shoulder:
    - If desired, trim any excess fat from the pork shoulder, leaving a thin layer for flavor and moisture.
    - Optional: Rub a thin layer of yellow mustard over the surface of the pork shoulder to help the dry rub adhere.
2. Apply the Dry Rub:
    - In a bowl, combine all the ingredients for the pork dry rub.
    - Generously rub the dry rub mixture all over the surface of the pork shoulder, ensuring it's evenly coated. Press the rub into the meat.
3. Prepare the Smoker:
    - Preheat your smoker to a temperature of 225-250°F (107-121°C).
    - Add wood chips or chunks (such as hickory, apple, cherry, or pecan) to the smoker box or tray.
4. Smoke the Pork Shoulder:
    - Place the seasoned pork shoulder directly on the smoker grate, fat side up.

- Close the smoker lid and maintain a consistent temperature throughout the smoking process.
- Plan for approximately 1.5 to 2 hours of smoking time per pound of pork shoulder, but smoking time can vary based on the size and thickness of the meat.

5. Monitor the Temperature:
   - Use a meat thermometer to monitor the internal temperature of the pork shoulder. The target temperature for pulled pork is around 195-205°F (90-96°C) for optimal tenderness.
   - After the pork shoulder reaches the desired temperature, it should be tender and easy to shred.

6. Rest and Serve:
   - Once done, carefully remove the smoked pork shoulder from the smoker and let it rest for about 30 minutes.
   - Use two forks to shred the smoked pork shoulder into pulled pork.
   - Serve the smoked pulled pork with barbecue sauce on sandwiches, tacos, or as a main dish with your favorite sides.

Tips:

- Keep the smoker temperature consistent throughout the smoking process to achieve even cooking.
- Allow enough time for the pork shoulder to smoke slowly and develop a smoky flavor.
- For additional flavor, you can use a combination of different wood chips or chunks.
- Customize the dry rub ingredients according to your taste preferences.

Smoking a pork shoulder is a rewarding cooking experience that yields tender, flavorful pulled pork. Enjoy the process and savor the delicious results! Adjust the smoking time based on the size and thickness of your pork shoulder for best results.

Smoked Beef Short Ribs

Ingredients:

- Beef short ribs, about 4-6 pieces (bone-in or boneless)
- Beef dry rub (see recipe below)
- Wood chips or chunks for smoking (hickory, oak, pecan, or mesquite)

Beef Dry Rub:

- 2 tablespoons brown sugar
- 1 tablespoon smoked paprika
- 1 tablespoon garlic powder
- 1 tablespoon onion powder
- 1 tablespoon kosher salt
- 1 teaspoon black pepper
- 1 teaspoon chili powder
- 1 teaspoon dried thyme

Instructions:

1. Prepare the Beef Short Ribs:
   - Rinse the beef short ribs under cold water and pat them dry with paper towels.
   - Trim any excess fat from the ribs, leaving a thin layer for flavor and moisture.
2. Apply the Beef Dry Rub:
   - In a small bowl, mix together all the ingredients for the beef dry rub.
   - Generously rub the dry rub mixture all over the surface of the beef short ribs, ensuring they are evenly coated. Press the rub into the meat.
3. Prepare the Smoker:
   - Preheat your smoker to a temperature of 225-250°F (107-121°C).
   - Add wood chips or chunks (such as hickory, oak, pecan, or mesquite) to the smoker box or tray.
4. Smoke the Beef Short Ribs:
   - Place the seasoned beef short ribs directly on the smoker grate, bone-side down.
   - Close the smoker lid and maintain a consistent temperature throughout the smoking process.

- Smoke the beef short ribs for approximately 4-6 hours, or until they reach an internal temperature of about 203°F (95°C) and the meat is tender and pulls away from the bone.

5. Wrap (Optional):
   - If desired, you can wrap the beef short ribs in butcher paper or foil halfway through the smoking process to help retain moisture and speed up the cooking time.
6. Rest and Serve:
   - Once the beef short ribs are done, carefully remove them from the smoker and let them rest for about 15-20 minutes.
   - Slice the smoked beef short ribs between the bones into individual portions.
7. Enjoy:
   - Serve the smoked beef short ribs hot as a main course with your favorite barbecue sauce and sides like coleslaw, baked beans, or cornbread.
   - The tender, smoky flavor of these beef short ribs will be a hit at any barbecue gathering!

Tips:

- Monitor the temperature of your smoker throughout the cooking process to ensure even smoking.
- Adjust the cooking time based on the thickness and size of the beef short ribs.
- Experiment with different wood chips or chunks to customize the flavor of your smoked beef short ribs.

Enjoy making and savoring these delicious smoked beef short ribs. The slow smoking process enhances the natural flavors of the meat and creates a memorable dining experience!

Smoked Sausages

Ingredients:

- Fresh sausages of your choice (such as bratwurst, Italian sausage, chorizo, etc.)
- Wood chips or chunks for smoking (applewood, hickory, cherry, or mesquite)
- Optional: BBQ sauce or mustard for serving

Instructions:

1. Preheat Your Smoker:
    - Preheat your smoker to a temperature of around 225-250°F (107-121°C). This low and slow cooking method will slowly cook the sausages while infusing them with smoky flavor.
2. Prepare the Sausages:
    - If using fresh uncooked sausages, prick each sausage a few times with a fork. This helps release excess fat and prevents them from bursting during smoking.
    - If using pre-cooked sausages, they can be smoked directly without any preparation.
3. Add Wood Chips or Chunks:
    - Add your desired wood chips or chunks (applewood, hickory, cherry, mesquite, etc.) to your smoker's wood chip tray or smoker box. This will generate the smoke needed to flavor the sausages.
4. Smoke the Sausages:
    - Place the sausages directly on the smoker grate, leaving space between them for the smoke to circulate.
    - Close the smoker lid and allow the sausages to smoke for about 1-2 hours, or until they reach an internal temperature of 160°F (71°C) for uncooked sausages, or until they are heated through for pre-cooked sausages.
5. Check and Rotate:
    - After about 30-45 minutes, check on the sausages and rotate them if necessary for even smoking.
6. Serve:
    - Once the sausages are fully cooked and infused with smoky flavor, remove them from the smoker.
    - Let the sausages rest for a few minutes before serving.
    - Serve the smoked sausages hot with your favorite condiments such as BBQ sauce, mustard, sauerkraut, or grilled onions and peppers.

Tips:

- Experiment with different types of wood chips or chunks to achieve different flavor profiles.
- Avoid overcooking the sausages, as they can become dry.
- If using pre-cooked sausages, adjust the smoking time to just infuse them with smoky flavor.
- Serve smoked sausages as a main dish with sides, in sandwiches, or as part of a charcuterie board.

Smoking sausages is a simple yet flavorful cooking method that adds depth to their taste. Enjoy the delicious smoky aroma and savor the juicy, flavorful sausages straight from the smoker! Adjust the smoking time based on the type and size of sausages you're using for the best results.

Smoked Meatloaf

Ingredients:

- 2 pounds ground beef (preferably 80/20 blend)
- 1 cup breadcrumbs (plain or seasoned)
- 2 eggs, beaten
- 1/2 cup diced onion
- 1/2 cup diced bell pepper (any color)
- 2 cloves garlic, minced
- 1/4 cup ketchup
- 2 tablespoons Worcestershire sauce
- 1 tablespoon Dijon mustard
- 1 tablespoon brown sugar
- 1 teaspoon salt
- 1/2 teaspoon black pepper
- Wood chips or chunks for smoking (hickory, apple, cherry, or oak)
- BBQ sauce (optional, for brushing)

Instructions:

1. Prepare the Meatloaf Mixture:
    - In a large mixing bowl, combine the ground beef, breadcrumbs, beaten eggs, diced onion, diced bell pepper, minced garlic, ketchup, Worcestershire sauce, Dijon mustard, brown sugar, salt, and black pepper.
    - Use your hands or a spoon to mix everything together until well combined. Avoid over-mixing to keep the meatloaf tender.
2. Shape the Meatloaf:
    - Form the meat mixture into a loaf shape on a sheet of aluminum foil or parchment paper. You can make one large loaf or divide the mixture into smaller loaves for individual servings.
3. Prepare the Smoker:
    - Preheat your smoker to a temperature of 225-250°F (107-121°C). Use wood chips or chunks (such as hickory, apple, cherry, or oak) for smoking.
4. Smoke the Meatloaf:
    - Place the formed meatloaf directly on the smoker grate.
    - Close the smoker lid and let the meatloaf smoke for approximately 2-3 hours, or until the internal temperature reaches 160°F (71°C) when measured with a meat thermometer inserted into the thickest part of the meatloaf.

- If desired, you can brush the meatloaf with BBQ sauce during the last 30 minutes of smoking for added flavor and caramelization.

5. Rest and Serve:
   - Once the smoked meatloaf is done, carefully remove it from the smoker and let it rest for about 10-15 minutes before slicing.
   - Slice the smoked meatloaf into thick slices and serve hot.
   - Enjoy your smoked meatloaf with mashed potatoes, roasted vegetables, or your favorite sides.

Tips:

- Feel free to customize the meatloaf mixture with additional ingredients such as chopped bacon, shredded cheese, or herbs.
- Make sure to use an accurate meat thermometer to ensure the meatloaf reaches a safe internal temperature.
- Leftover smoked meatloaf can be refrigerated and enjoyed for several days. Reheat slices in the microwave or oven for a quick and tasty meal.

Smoking meatloaf adds a wonderful depth of flavor that elevates this classic dish. Enjoy the smoky goodness and savory taste of smoked meatloaf for a memorable meal! Adjust the smoking time based on the size and thickness of your meatloaf for the best results.

Smoked Stuffed Peppers

Ingredients:

- Bell peppers (any color), tops cut off and seeds removed
- 1 pound ground beef or turkey
- 1 cup cooked rice (white or brown)
- 1 onion, finely chopped
- 2 cloves garlic, minced
- 1 can (14.5 oz) diced tomatoes, drained
- 1 cup shredded cheese (such as cheddar or mozzarella)
- 1 tablespoon Worcestershire sauce
- 1 teaspoon dried oregano
- 1 teaspoon dried basil
- Salt and pepper, to taste
- Olive oil

Instructions:

1. Prepare the Bell Peppers:
    - Cut the tops off the bell peppers and remove the seeds and membranes from inside.
    - Lightly brush the outside of the peppers with olive oil.
2. Prepare the Filling:
    - In a skillet, heat a drizzle of olive oil over medium heat.
    - Add the chopped onion and garlic, and sauté until softened.
    - Add the ground beef or turkey to the skillet and cook until browned.
    - Drain any excess fat from the skillet.
    - Stir in the cooked rice, drained diced tomatoes, Worcestershire sauce, dried oregano, dried basil, salt, and pepper.
    - Cook for another 2-3 minutes to combine and heat through.
    - Remove the skillet from heat and let the filling cool slightly.
3. Preheat the Smoker:
    - Preheat your smoker to a temperature of 225-250°F (107-121°C) using wood chips or chunks (such as hickory, apple, cherry, or oak) for smoking.
4. Stuff the Peppers:
    - Fill each bell pepper with the meat and rice filling, pressing down gently to pack the filling.
    - Top each stuffed pepper with shredded cheese if desired.
5. Smoke the Stuffed Peppers:

- Place the stuffed peppers directly on the smoker grate or in a grill-safe pan.
- Close the smoker lid and smoke the stuffed peppers for about 2-3 hours, or until the peppers are tender and the filling is heated through.
- If using a thermometer, ensure the internal temperature of the filling reaches 160°F (71°C).

6. Serve:
    - Carefully remove the smoked stuffed peppers from the smoker.
    - Serve the smoked stuffed peppers hot, garnished with chopped fresh herbs if desired.

Tips:

- Feel free to customize the filling with your favorite ingredients such as diced mushrooms, corn, black beans, or spinach.
- You can also use different types of cheese for topping, such as Monterey Jack or pepper jack for a spicy kick.
- Leftover smoked stuffed peppers can be refrigerated and reheated for a delicious meal the next day.

Smoked stuffed peppers are a fantastic dish that showcases the wonderful flavor of smoked meats and vegetables. Enjoy these flavorful stuffed peppers as a main course or as a side dish alongside your favorite barbecue fare! Adjust the smoking time based on the size and thickness of your peppers for optimal results.

Smoked Meatballs

Ingredients:

- 1 pound ground beef (or a mixture of beef and pork)
- 1/2 cup breadcrumbs
- 1/4 cup grated Parmesan cheese
- 1 egg
- 2 cloves garlic, minced
- 1 teaspoon dried oregano
- 1 teaspoon dried basil
- 1/2 teaspoon salt
- 1/4 teaspoon black pepper
- Wood chips or chunks for smoking (hickory, apple, cherry, or maple)
- Marinara sauce (for serving, optional)

Instructions:

1. Prepare the Meatball Mixture:
    - In a large mixing bowl, combine the ground beef, breadcrumbs, Parmesan cheese, egg, minced garlic, dried oregano, dried basil, salt, and black pepper.
    - Use your hands or a spoon to mix everything together until well combined.
2. Shape the Meatballs:
    - Roll the meat mixture into small meatballs, about 1 inch in diameter. You should be able to make approximately 24 meatballs from the mixture.
3. Preheat the Smoker:
    - Preheat your smoker to a temperature of 225-250°F (107-121°C) using wood chips or chunks (such as hickory, apple, cherry, or maple) for smoking.
4. Smoke the Meatballs:
    - Place the shaped meatballs directly on the smoker grate, leaving space between them for the smoke to circulate.
    - Close the smoker lid and smoke the meatballs for about 1.5-2 hours, or until they reach an internal temperature of 160°F (71°C) when measured with a meat thermometer.
5. Serve:
    - Once the smoked meatballs are done, remove them from the smoker.
    - Serve the smoked meatballs hot as appetizers with marinara sauce for dipping, or add them to pasta dishes, sandwiches, or soups.

Tips:

- For added flavor, you can mix in chopped fresh herbs like parsley or basil into the meatball mixture.
- If you prefer a smokier flavor, you can extend the smoking time slightly, but be careful not to overcook the meatballs.
- Leftover smoked meatballs can be refrigerated and reheated in the oven or microwave for quick meals.

Smoked meatballs are a delicious and savory treat that's sure to be a hit at any gathering. Enjoy the rich, smoky flavor of these meatballs served in your favorite way! Adjust the smoking time based on the size of your meatballs and your preferred level of smokiness.

Smoked Pork Belly

Ingredients:

- 2-3 pounds pork belly, skin-on or skinless
- Pork dry rub or seasoning (see recipe below)
- Wood chips or chunks for smoking (hickory, apple, cherry, or maple)

Pork Dry Rub or Seasoning:

- 2 tablespoons brown sugar
- 1 tablespoon paprika
- 1 tablespoon garlic powder
- 1 tablespoon onion powder
- 1 tablespoon kosher salt
- 1 teaspoon black pepper
- 1 teaspoon dried thyme
- 1 teaspoon dried rosemary

Instructions:

1. Prepare the Pork Belly:
    - If the pork belly has skin on, you can choose to remove it or leave it on based on your preference. Score the skin with a sharp knife in a cross-hatch pattern if leaving it on.
2. Apply the Dry Rub:
    - In a small bowl, mix together all the ingredients for the pork dry rub or seasoning.
    - Rub the dry rub mixture all over the surface of the pork belly, ensuring it's evenly coated. If possible, apply the rub a few hours before smoking to allow the flavors to penetrate the meat.
3. Preheat the Smoker:
    - Preheat your smoker to a temperature of 225-250°F (107-121°C) using wood chips or chunks (such as hickory, apple, cherry, or maple) for smoking.
4. Smoke the Pork Belly:
    - Place the seasoned pork belly directly on the smoker grate, with the fat side up.

- Close the smoker lid and smoke the pork belly for approximately 3-4 hours, or until the internal temperature reaches about 195-203°F (90-95°C) when measured with a meat thermometer inserted into the thickest part of the meat.
- The pork belly should be tender and easily pierced with a fork.

5. Rest and Serve:
    - Once the smoked pork belly is done, remove it from the smoker and let it rest for about 10-15 minutes before slicing.
    - Slice the smoked pork belly into thick slices or cubes, depending on your preference.
6. Optional: Crisp the Skin (if applicable):
    - If you kept the skin on the pork belly and want to crisp it up, you can place the slices under a broiler for a few minutes until the skin becomes crispy.
7. Enjoy:
    - Serve the smoked pork belly slices as a main dish with sides like coleslaw, roasted vegetables, or mashed potatoes.
    - Alternatively, use the smoked pork belly in tacos, sandwiches, or salads for a deliciously smoky flavor.

Tips:

- For extra flavor, you can marinate the pork belly in a simple brine or marinade before applying the dry rub.
- Adjust the smoking time based on the thickness of your pork belly and your desired level of doneness.
- Leftover smoked pork belly can be refrigerated and reheated gently in the oven or skillet for future meals.

Smoked pork belly is a decadent and flavorful dish that's perfect for special occasions or anytime you want to indulge in some delicious smoked meat. Enjoy the melt-in-your-mouth texture and rich smoky taste of this smoked pork belly recipe!

Smoked Duck Breast

Ingredients:

- Duck breasts (skin-on or skinless)
- Salt and pepper, to taste
- Optional: Duck dry rub or seasoning (see recipe below)
- Wood chips or chunks for smoking (applewood, cherry, hickory, or oak)

Duck Dry Rub or Seasoning (optional):

- 2 tablespoons brown sugar
- 1 tablespoon paprika
- 1 teaspoon garlic powder
- 1 teaspoon onion powder
- 1 teaspoon dried thyme
- 1 teaspoon dried rosemary
- Salt and pepper, to taste

Instructions:

1. Prepare the Duck Breasts:
    - Pat the duck breasts dry with paper towels.
    - Score the skin of the duck breasts with a sharp knife in a cross-hatch pattern, being careful not to cut into the meat.
    - Season both sides of the duck breasts with salt and pepper. Optionally, you can use a duck dry rub or seasoning for additional flavor.
2. Preheat the Smoker:
    - Preheat your smoker to a temperature of 225-250°F (107-121°C) using wood chips or chunks (such as applewood, cherry, hickory, or oak) for smoking.
3. Smoke the Duck Breasts:
    - Place the seasoned duck breasts directly on the smoker grate, skin-side up.
    - Close the smoker lid and smoke the duck breasts for approximately 1.5 to 2 hours, or until the internal temperature reaches about 135-140°F (57-60°C) for medium-rare or 150°F (65°C) for medium when measured with a meat thermometer inserted into the thickest part of the meat.

- The duck breasts should develop a beautiful golden-brown color and a smoky aroma.
4. Rest and Serve:
   - Once the smoked duck breasts reach your desired doneness, remove them from the smoker and let them rest for about 10 minutes before slicing.
   - Slice the smoked duck breasts thinly against the grain.
5. Enjoy:
   - Serve the smoked duck breast slices as a main course with a side of wild rice, roasted vegetables, or a fruit compote.
   - Alternatively, use the smoked duck breast in salads, sandwiches, or pasta dishes for a delicious smoky flavor.

Tips:

- Adjust the smoking time based on the size and thickness of your duck breasts.
- Avoid overcooking the duck breasts to preserve their tenderness and juiciness.
- Duck pairs well with sweet and savory flavors, so consider serving with a fruit-based sauce or glaze.

Smoking duck breast is a wonderful way to enjoy this flavorful and versatile meat. The smoky aroma and tender texture make it a perfect choice for special occasions or everyday meals. Experiment with different wood flavors and seasonings to customize your smoked duck breast to your liking!

Smoked Beef Jerky

Ingredients:

- 2 pounds beef (such as flank steak or sirloin), thinly sliced against the grain
- For the marinade:
    - 1 cup soy sauce
    - 1/4 cup Worcestershire sauce
    - 2 tablespoons honey or maple syrup
    - 2 teaspoons onion powder
    - 2 teaspoons garlic powder
    - 1 teaspoon black pepper
    - 1 teaspoon smoked paprika (optional, for additional smoky flavor)
    - 1/2 teaspoon cayenne pepper (adjust to taste for spiciness)
- Wood chips or chunks for smoking (hickory, mesquite, applewood, cherry, etc.)

Instructions:

1. Prepare the Beef:
    - Start with a lean cut of beef (flank steak or sirloin) and slice it thinly against the grain. Aim for slices about 1/8 to 1/4 inch thick for best results.
2. Make the Marinade:
    - In a bowl, whisk together the soy sauce, Worcestershire sauce, honey or maple syrup, onion powder, garlic powder, black pepper, smoked paprika (if using), and cayenne pepper.
    - Place the sliced beef in a large resealable plastic bag or container, and pour the marinade over the beef, ensuring all pieces are coated. Seal the bag or cover the container, and refrigerate for at least 4 hours or overnight to marinate.
3. Preheat the Smoker:
    - Preheat your smoker to a low temperature (around 180-200°F or 82-93°C). Use wood chips or chunks (hickory, mesquite, applewood, cherry, etc.) for smoking.
4. Prepare the Beef Jerky for Smoking:
    - Remove the marinated beef slices from the refrigerator and pat them dry with paper towels to remove excess marinade.
    - Arrange the beef slices in a single layer on the smoker racks, making sure they are not overlapping.
5. Smoke the Beef Jerky:

- Place the beef jerky in the preheated smoker.
- Smoke the beef jerky for approximately 3-4 hours, or until it reaches your desired level of dryness and chewiness. Rotate or flip the beef slices halfway through the smoking process for even cooking.

6. Check for Doneness:
   - The beef jerky is ready when it is dry to the touch but still flexible, with a deep smoky flavor. It should bend without breaking.
7. Cool and Store:
   - Once smoked, let the beef jerky cool completely before storing.
   - Store the smoked beef jerky in an airtight container or resealable bags. It can be kept at room temperature for a few days, or refrigerated for longer shelf life.

Tips:

- For easier slicing, partially freeze the beef before slicing thinly.
- Customize the marinade to your taste preferences by adjusting the level of sweetness, spiciness, or smokiness.
- Feel free to experiment with different wood flavors for smoking to create unique flavor profiles for your beef jerky.

Homemade smoked beef jerky is a delicious and satisfying snack that's perfect for hiking, camping, or enjoying at home. The smoky, savory flavor of homemade beef jerky beats store-bought versions any day! Adjust the smoking time based on the thickness of your beef slices and your desired level of chewiness for the best results.

Smoked Pork Chops

Ingredients:

- Pork chops (bone-in or boneless)
- Salt
- Pepper
- Paprika
- Garlic powder
- Onion powder
- Liquid smoke (optional)
- Olive oil

Instructions:

1. Prepare the Pork Chops:
    - Start with fresh pork chops. You can use bone-in or boneless chops depending on your preference.
    - Trim excess fat from the edges of the chops if desired.
2. Seasoning:
    - In a small bowl, mix salt, pepper, paprika, garlic powder, and onion powder to create a dry rub.
    - Rub the dry seasoning mixture generously over the pork chops. Ensure both sides are well coated.
3. Marinate (Optional Step):
    - For added flavor, you can marinate the pork chops in a mixture of olive oil and liquid smoke. Place the seasoned chops in a dish, drizzle with olive oil and a few dashes of liquid smoke, then cover and refrigerate for at least 1 hour (or overnight).
4. Preheat the Smoker:
    - Prepare your smoker according to the manufacturer's instructions. Aim for a temperature of around 225-250°F (107-121°C).
5. Smoking:
    - Once the smoker is ready, place the seasoned pork chops directly on the grate.
    - Close the lid and smoke the pork chops for about 1.5 to 2 hours, or until they reach an internal temperature of 145°F (63°C) for medium doneness.
6. Serve:
    - Once done, remove the smoked pork chops from the smoker and let them rest for a few minutes before serving.
    - Serve the smoked pork chops with your favorite sides like mashed potatoes, coleslaw, or grilled vegetables.

Tips:

- Use a meat thermometer to ensure the pork chops are cooked to the right internal temperature.

- You can customize the dry rub by adding other spices like cayenne pepper, thyme, or brown sugar for a sweeter profile.
- Experiment with different wood chips or chunks in your smoker (such as applewood or hickory) to impart unique flavors to the pork chops.

Enjoy your homemade smoked pork chops!

Smoked Shrimp

Ingredients:

- Fresh shrimp, peeled and deveined (leave tails on for presentation if desired)
- Olive oil
- Salt
- Pepper
- Garlic powder
- Paprika
- Lemon wedges (for serving)

Instructions:

1. Prepare the Shrimp:
    - Ensure the shrimp are cleaned, peeled, and deveined. Pat them dry with paper towels.
2. Seasoning:
    - In a bowl, mix olive oil with salt, pepper, garlic powder, and paprika. Adjust the seasoning quantities based on your taste preference.
3. Coat the Shrimp:
    - Toss the shrimp in the seasoned olive oil mixture, ensuring each shrimp is well coated.
4. Preheat the Smoker:
    - Prepare your smoker for cooking at a temperature of around 225-250°F (107-121°C). Use wood chips or chunks suitable for seafood, such as fruit woods like apple or cherry.
5. Smoking the Shrimp:
    - Arrange the seasoned shrimp in a single layer on a grill rack or a perforated smoker pan.
    - Place the shrimp in the smoker once it reaches the desired temperature.
    - Smoke the shrimp for about 20-30 minutes. The cooking time will depend on the size of the shrimp and the temperature of your smoker. The shrimp should turn pink and opaque when done.
6. Serve:
    - Remove the smoked shrimp from the smoker and let them rest for a few minutes.
    - Serve the smoked shrimp hot or at room temperature with lemon wedges on the side for squeezing over the shrimp.

Tips:

- Don't overcook the shrimp, as they can become rubbery. Keep an eye on them and remove them from the smoker once they're pink and opaque.
- You can add additional flavors to the olive oil mixture, such as minced fresh garlic, chopped herbs (like parsley or dill), or a splash of hot sauce for some heat.
- Serve smoked shrimp as an appetizer or as part of a seafood platter alongside cocktail sauce or aioli.

Enjoy your delicious smoked shrimp with its unique smoky flavor that complements the natural sweetness of the seafood!

Smoked Mac and Cheese

Ingredients:

- 1 lb (450g) elbow macaroni or pasta of your choice
- 4 cups (946ml) whole milk
- 1/2 cup (113g) unsalted butter
- 1/2 cup (60g) all-purpose flour
- 4 cups (about 400g) shredded cheese (such as sharp cheddar, Gruyère, or a mix of your favorite cheeses)
- Salt and pepper, to taste
- 1/2 teaspoon smoked paprika
- Optional add-ins (crumbled bacon, diced jalapeños, chopped herbs, etc.)
- Breadcrumbs (for topping)
- Olive oil (for drizzling)
- Wood chips for smoking (hickory, applewood, or your preferred smoking wood)

Instructions:

1. Cook the Pasta:
    - Cook the elbow macaroni or pasta according to the package instructions until al dente. Drain and set aside.
2. Prepare the Cheese Sauce:
    - In a large saucepan, melt the butter over medium heat.
    - Add the flour and whisk continuously to make a roux. Cook for 1-2 minutes until the roux is golden and fragrant.
    - Gradually pour in the milk while whisking constantly to avoid lumps.
    - Cook the sauce, stirring frequently, until it thickens and coats the back of a spoon.
    - Remove the saucepan from the heat and stir in the shredded cheese until melted and smooth.
    - Season the cheese sauce with salt, pepper, and smoked paprika to taste.
3. Combine Pasta and Cheese Sauce:
    - Add the cooked pasta to the cheese sauce, stirring until the pasta is well coated with the cheesy goodness.
    - If desired, stir in any optional add-ins like bacon, jalapeños, or herbs.
4. Prepare the Smoker:
    - Preheat your smoker to 225-250°F (107-121°C) using your preferred smoking wood chips.
5. Smoke the Mac and Cheese:

- Transfer the mac and cheese to a disposable aluminum pan or a heat-proof dish suitable for smoking.
- Place the pan in the smoker once it reaches the desired temperature.
- Close the smoker and smoke the mac and cheese for about 1-1.5 hours. The longer it smokes, the more intense the smoky flavor will be.

6. Add Breadcrumb Topping (Optional):
    - If you like a crunchy topping, mix breadcrumbs with a drizzle of olive oil and sprinkle them over the mac and cheese during the last 15-20 minutes of smoking.
7. Serve and Enjoy:
    - Once the mac and cheese is nicely smoked and heated through, remove it from the smoker.
    - Let it rest for a few minutes before serving to allow the flavors to meld together.
    - Serve the smoked mac and cheese hot as a delicious and smoky side dish or main course.

Tips:

- Experiment with different types of cheese to create your favorite flavor combination.
- Customize the add-ins based on your preferences—try adding cooked lobster meat, roasted vegetables, or different spices for variety.
- Keep an eye on the mac and cheese while smoking to prevent it from drying out. If it starts to look dry, cover it loosely with foil during the smoking process.

Enjoy your homemade smoked mac and cheese with its irresistible smoky-cheesy goodness!

Smoked Corn on the Cob

Ingredients:

- Fresh corn on the cob, husked
- Butter, softened
- Salt and pepper, to taste
- Optional: Herbs like chopped parsley or cilantro, grated Parmesan cheese, chili powder, or smoked paprika

Instructions:

1. Preparation:
    - Start by husking the corn and removing the silk. Rinse the corn under cold water to remove any remaining silk strands.
2. Seasoning:
    - Spread softened butter evenly over each ear of corn. You can use a brush or your hands to coat the corn thoroughly.
    - Season the corn with salt and pepper. Optionally, sprinkle with herbs, grated Parmesan cheese, or spices like chili powder or smoked paprika for extra flavor.
3. Preheat the Smoker:
    - Preheat your smoker to a temperature of around 225-250°F (107-121°C). Use your choice of smoking wood chips or chunks (such as hickory, applewood, or mesquite) for flavor.
4. Smoking the Corn:
    - Arrange the seasoned corn directly on the smoker grate or in a smoker-safe pan.
    - Close the lid of the smoker and let the corn smoke for about 30-45 minutes. The exact cooking time will depend on the temperature of your smoker and the desired level of smokiness.
5. Check for Doneness:
    - After about 30 minutes, check the corn. It should be tender and cooked through, with a slightly smoky aroma and flavor.
6. Serve:
    - Remove the smoked corn from the smoker and let it cool slightly.
    - Serve the smoked corn on the cob as is, or with additional butter and seasoning if desired.

Tips:

- Experiment with different types of seasoning to customize the flavor of your smoked corn. Garlic powder, lime juice, and cotija cheese are other delicious options to try.
- For added richness, you can wrap each ear of corn with a slice of bacon before smoking.
- If you prefer a charred finish, you can briefly grill the smoked corn over direct heat on a barbecue grill after smoking.

Enjoy your delicious smoked corn on the cob, bursting with smoky-sweet flavor! It makes a perfect side dish for summer cookouts and BBQs.

Smoked Meat Pizza

Ingredients:

For the Pizza Dough:

- 1 pound (450g) pizza dough, homemade or store-bought
- Cornmeal or flour (for dusting)

For the Pizza Toppings:

- 1 cup pizza sauce
- 2 cups shredded mozzarella cheese (or a blend of cheeses like provolone and Parmesan)
- Smoked meat of your choice (e.g., smoked sausage, pulled pork, smoked chicken, or smoked brisket), sliced or shredded
- Sliced bell peppers, onions, mushrooms, or any other desired vegetables
- Olive oil
- Salt, pepper, and Italian seasoning (to taste)
- Optional: Fresh basil leaves or parsley, chopped (for garnish)

Instructions:

1. Preheat Your Smoker:
    - Preheat your smoker to a temperature of around 400°F (200°C). Use a combination of wood chips like hickory, apple, or cherry for a smoky flavor.
2. Prepare the Pizza Dough:
    - If using store-bought dough, let it come to room temperature. If making homemade dough, roll it out on a lightly floured surface into your desired pizza shape (round or rectangular).
    - Transfer the rolled-out dough onto a pizza peel or a parchment-lined baking sheet dusted with cornmeal or flour to prevent sticking.
3. Assemble the Pizza:
    - Spread the pizza sauce evenly over the dough, leaving a small border around the edges for the crust.
    - Sprinkle the shredded mozzarella cheese over the sauce.
4. Add the Smoked Meat and Toppings:
    - Distribute the sliced or shredded smoked meat over the cheese.

- Scatter sliced bell peppers, onions, mushrooms, or any other desired vegetables over the pizza.
5. Season and Drizzle:
    - Drizzle a little olive oil over the pizza and season with salt, pepper, and Italian seasoning to taste.
6. Transfer to the Smoker:
    - Carefully transfer the assembled pizza onto the preheated smoker grate or a pizza stone in the smoker.
7. Smoke and Bake:
    - Close the lid of the smoker and let the pizza cook for about 10-15 minutes, or until the cheese is melted and bubbly, and the crust is golden brown.
    - Keep an eye on the pizza to prevent burning. Cooking times may vary depending on the heat of your smoker.
8. Finish and Serve:
    - Once done, carefully remove the smoked meat pizza from the smoker.
    - If desired, sprinkle chopped fresh basil or parsley over the top for added freshness and flavor.
    - Let the pizza rest for a few minutes before slicing and serving.

Tips:

- Customize your smoked meat pizza with your favorite smoked meats and vegetables.
- You can use leftover smoked meats from a previous barbecue session for extra flavor.
- Experiment with different cheese blends and seasonings to suit your taste preferences.
- Serve the smoked meat pizza hot alongside a fresh salad for a complete meal.

Enjoy your homemade smoked meat pizza, packed with delicious smoky flavors and perfect for any occasion!

Smoked Stuffed Mushrooms

Ingredients:

- Large white or cremini mushrooms, cleaned and stems removed (about 20-24 mushrooms)
- Olive oil
- Salt and pepper, to taste
- 8 oz (225g) cream cheese, softened
- 1/2 cup grated Parmesan cheese
- 2 cloves garlic, minced
- 2 green onions, finely chopped
- 1/4 cup breadcrumbs (plain or seasoned)
- Fresh parsley, chopped (for garnish)
- Optional: Cooked and crumbled bacon or finely chopped cooked sausage

Instructions:

1. Prepare the Mushrooms:
    - Preheat your smoker to a temperature of around 225-250°F (107-121°C) using your preferred smoking wood chips or chunks (such as applewood, hickory, or oak).
    - Clean the mushrooms with a damp cloth to remove any dirt. Remove the stems by gently twisting them off, creating a hollow cavity in each mushroom cap. Set aside.
2. Prepare the Filling:
    - In a mixing bowl, combine the softened cream cheese, grated Parmesan cheese, minced garlic, chopped green onions, breadcrumbs, and optional cooked and crumbled bacon or sausage.
    - Season the filling mixture with salt and pepper to taste. Stir until well combined.
3. Stuff the Mushrooms:
    - Using a small spoon or your fingers, stuff each mushroom cap with a generous amount of the cream cheese filling mixture, mounding it slightly.
4. Arrange in the Smoker:
    - Place the stuffed mushrooms on a wire rack or directly on the smoker grate, ensuring they are spaced apart for even smoking.
5. Smoke the Mushrooms:
    - Place the mushrooms in the preheated smoker and close the lid.

- Smoke the stuffed mushrooms for about 60-90 minutes, or until the mushrooms are tender and the filling is golden brown and slightly bubbly.
6. Serve and Garnish:
    - Carefully remove the smoked stuffed mushrooms from the smoker.
    - Garnish with freshly chopped parsley for a pop of color and freshness.
7. Serve Warm:
    - Arrange the smoked stuffed mushrooms on a serving platter and serve them warm as a delicious appetizer or party snack.

Tips:

- Customize the filling by adding your favorite ingredients like chopped spinach, sun-dried tomatoes, or different types of cheese.
- If you prefer a stronger smoky flavor, use a more robust smoking wood like hickory or mesquite.
- Make sure not to overfill the mushrooms to prevent the filling from spilling out during smoking.

Enjoy these smoky, savory smoked stuffed mushrooms at your next gathering or as a tasty appetizer before a meal. They are sure to be a hit with mushroom lovers and non-mushroom lovers alike!

Smoked Lamb Ribs

Ingredients:

- Lamb ribs (approximately 2-3 pounds)
- Olive oil
- Salt and pepper, to taste
- Your favorite dry rub or seasoning blend (e.g., garlic powder, onion powder, paprika, cumin, chili powder)
- Wood chips for smoking (e.g., applewood, cherry wood, hickory)

Instructions:

1. Prepare the Lamb Ribs:
    - Start by trimming any excess fat from the lamb ribs. Remove the membrane on the bone side of the ribs for better seasoning penetration.
2. Season the Ribs:
    - Drizzle the lamb ribs with olive oil and rub them all over to coat evenly.
    - Season the ribs generously with salt, pepper, and your favorite dry rub or seasoning blend. Ensure the ribs are well coated on all sides.
3. Preheat the Smoker:
    - Preheat your smoker to a temperature of about 225-250°F (107-121°C). Use your preferred wood chips or chunks for smoking lamb (fruitwoods like apple or cherry work well).
4. Smoke the Lamb Ribs:
    - Place the seasoned lamb ribs directly on the smoker grate, bone side down.
    - Close the lid of the smoker and let the ribs smoke for approximately 3-4 hours, depending on the size of the ribs and desired level of tenderness. Aim for an internal temperature of around 195-203°F (90-95°C) for a tender result.
    - Add more wood chips or chunks to the smoker as needed to maintain a steady smoke.
5. Check for Doneness:
    - After a few hours of smoking, check the internal temperature of the lamb ribs using a meat thermometer. They should be tender and easily pull apart.
6. Rest and Serve:
    - Once done, remove the smoked lamb ribs from the smoker and let them rest for about 10-15 minutes.

- Slice the ribs between the bones and serve hot. Optionally, brush them with a bit of barbecue sauce or glaze before serving.

Tips:

- Lamb ribs can vary in size, so adjust the smoking time accordingly. Larger ribs may require additional smoking time.
- For added flavor, marinate the lamb ribs in a herb-infused olive oil mixture before applying the dry rub.
- Serve smoked lamb ribs with your favorite sides like roasted vegetables, mashed potatoes, or a fresh salad.

Enjoy your mouthwatering smoked lamb ribs, showcasing the delicious marriage of lamb and smoky flavors from the smoker!

Smoked Tofu

Ingredients:

- Firm tofu
- Olive oil or vegetable oil
- Soy sauce (or tamari for gluten-free option)
- Liquid smoke (optional)
- Salt and pepper, to taste
- Your favorite spices or seasonings (e.g., garlic powder, paprika, chili powder)

Instructions:

1. Preparation:
    - Start by pressing the tofu to remove excess moisture. Place the block of tofu between paper towels or clean kitchen towels, and place a heavy object (like a cast iron skillet or books) on top. Let it press for about 30 minutes to an hour.
2. Marinate the Tofu:
    - In a bowl, whisk together olive oil (or vegetable oil), soy sauce (or tamari), liquid smoke (if using), salt, pepper, and any additional spices or seasonings of your choice.
    - Cut the pressed tofu into slices or cubes, depending on your preference.
3. Coat with Marinade:
    - Place the tofu pieces in a shallow dish or a resealable plastic bag. Pour the marinade over the tofu, ensuring all pieces are well coated. Let the tofu marinate for at least 30 minutes, or longer for more flavor.
4. Prepare the Smoker:
    - Preheat your smoker to a temperature of about 225-250°F (107-121°C). Use your choice of smoking wood chips or chunks (such as hickory, applewood, or mesquite) for flavor.
5. Smoke the Tofu:
    - Arrange the marinated tofu pieces on a wire rack or directly on the smoker grate.
    - Place the tofu in the smoker once it reaches the desired temperature.
    - Close the lid of the smoker and let the tofu smoke for about 1-2 hours, depending on the level of smokiness desired. Turn the tofu pieces halfway through the smoking process for even smoking.
6. Check for Doneness:

- After smoking, the tofu should have a golden-brown color and a firm texture. Taste a piece to ensure it has absorbed enough smoky flavor.
7. Serve or Store:
   - Once done, remove the smoked tofu from the smoker and let it cool slightly.
   - Enjoy the smoked tofu as a standalone snack, or use it in salads, sandwiches, stir-fries, or other dishes.

Tips:

- Adjust the amount of liquid smoke based on your preference for smokiness.
- Experiment with different spices and seasonings in the marinade to create unique flavor profiles.
- Store leftover smoked tofu in an airtight container in the refrigerator for up to a few days. Use it cold or reheated in various dishes.

Smoked tofu adds depth and complexity to vegetarian and vegan recipes, providing a smoky element that pairs well with a variety of flavors. Enjoy your homemade smoked tofu in creative culinary creations!

Smoked Sweet Potatoes

Ingredients:

- Sweet potatoes (choose medium to large-sized potatoes)
- Olive oil
- Salt
- Optional toppings: Butter, brown sugar, cinnamon, chopped herbs (e.g., parsley or thyme), or a sprinkle of smoked paprika

Instructions:

1. Preparation:
    - Wash the sweet potatoes thoroughly under running water to remove any dirt or debris. Pat them dry with paper towels.
2. Preheat the Smoker:
    - Preheat your smoker to a temperature of about 225-250°F (107-121°C). Use your preferred smoking wood chips or chunks (such as applewood, hickory, or maple) for flavor.
3. Prepare the Sweet Potatoes:
    - Pierce each sweet potato several times with a fork to allow steam to escape during smoking. This prevents them from bursting.
4. Coat with Olive Oil and Salt:
    - Rub each sweet potato with olive oil to coat evenly. Sprinkle salt all over the sweet potatoes.
5. Smoke the Sweet Potatoes:
    - Place the prepared sweet potatoes directly on the smoker grate.
    - Close the lid of the smoker and let the sweet potatoes smoke for approximately 2-3 hours, depending on their size. They are ready when they are tender and can be easily pierced with a fork.
6. Serve and Enjoy:
    - Remove the smoked sweet potatoes from the smoker and let them cool slightly.
    - Cut open each sweet potato and fluff the flesh with a fork.
    - Serve the smoked sweet potatoes hot with optional toppings like butter, brown sugar, cinnamon, chopped herbs, or a sprinkle of smoked paprika.

Tips:

- For extra flavor, you can add a pat of butter or sprinkle of brown sugar inside each sweet potato before serving.
- Experiment with different seasonings or toppings to customize the flavor of your smoked sweet potatoes.
- Smoked sweet potatoes can be served as a side dish or incorporated into various recipes like salads, soups, or casseroles.

Smoking sweet potatoes adds a delicious smoky twist to this versatile and nutritious vegetable. Enjoy the unique flavor of smoked sweet potatoes in your favorite dishes!

Smoked Cheese

Ingredients and Equipment:

- Block(s) of cheese (choose varieties like cheddar, gouda, mozzarella, or provolone)
- Smoking wood chips or pellets (use mild woods like apple, cherry, or pecan)
- Smoker (electric, charcoal, or pellet smoker)
- Aluminum foil or smoker tray
- Thermometer (optional)

Instructions:

1. Choose the Right Cheese:
    - Select cheeses that are firm and can hold their shape well when smoked. Good options include cheddar, gouda, mozzarella, provolone, or even block cream cheese.
2. Prep the Cheese:
    - Cut the cheese into blocks or smaller pieces for easier smoking. Aim for pieces that are about 1-inch thick.
3. Prep the Smoker:
    - Preheat your smoker to a very low temperature, ideally around 90-100°F (32-38°C). The goal is to use the smoker as a cold smoker to avoid melting the cheese.
4. Prepare the Smoking Setup:
    - If using an electric or pellet smoker, set it up for cold smoking. If using a charcoal smoker, light a small amount of charcoal and add unlit charcoal along with wood chips or pellets to generate smoke without much heat.
5. Smoke the Cheese:
    - Place the cheese pieces on a wire rack, cheese grates, or in a shallow pan inside the smoker.
    - If using a charcoal smoker, keep the smoker's temperature as low as possible by controlling airflow and adding minimal charcoal or wood.
6. Add Smoke Flavor:
    - Place the wood chips or pellets in the smoker according to the manufacturer's instructions. Let the cheese absorb the smoke for about 1-3 hours, depending on how smoky you want it to be. The longer you smoke, the deeper the flavor.
7. Monitor the Temperature:

- Use a thermometer to monitor the internal temperature of the smoker and ensure it stays low. The cheese should not exceed 90-100°F (32-38°C) to prevent melting.
8. Finish and Store:
    - Once smoked to your liking, remove the cheese from the smoker.
    - Let the smoked cheese rest at room temperature for about 30 minutes to allow the flavors to settle.
    - Wrap the smoked cheese tightly in plastic wrap or vacuum-sealed bags and refrigerate for at least 24 hours before consuming. This allows the flavors to mellow and develop.

Tips:

- Experiment with different cheese varieties and wood types to create unique flavor combinations.
- Smoked cheese pairs well with crackers, bread, fruits, and charcuterie.
- Store smoked cheese in the refrigerator and consume within a few weeks for optimal freshness.

Enjoy your homemade smoked cheese as a delicious snack or ingredient in various recipes. The subtle smoky flavor will add a gourmet touch to your culinary creations!

Smoked Pork Tenderloin

Ingredients:

- 2 pork tenderloins (about 1 to 1.5 pounds each)
- Olive oil
- Dry rub or seasoning blend (e.g., salt, pepper, garlic powder, onion powder, paprika, brown sugar)
- Wood chips or chunks for smoking (hickory, applewood, cherry, or a combination)

Instructions:

1. Prep the Pork Tenderloins:
    - Trim any excess fat or silver skin from the pork tenderloins. Pat them dry with paper towels.
2. Season the Tenderloins:
    - Drizzle a little olive oil over the pork tenderloins and rub them to coat evenly.
    - Generously season the tenderloins with your favorite dry rub or seasoning blend. Ensure all sides are well coated.
3. Preheat the Smoker:
    - Preheat your smoker to a temperature of about 225-250°F (107-121°C). Use your choice of smoking wood chips or chunks for flavor.
4. Smoke the Pork Tenderloins:
    - Place the seasoned pork tenderloins directly on the smoker grate.
    - Close the lid of the smoker and let the pork tenderloins smoke for approximately 1.5 to 2 hours, or until they reach an internal temperature of about 145°F (63°C) for medium doneness. You can smoke them to a higher temperature for more well-done meat if preferred.
5. Monitor the Temperature:
    - Use a meat thermometer to monitor the internal temperature of the pork tenderloins. Insert the thermometer into the thickest part of the meat to get an accurate reading.
6. Rest and Slice:
    - Once the pork tenderloins reach the desired temperature, remove them from the smoker and transfer them to a cutting board.
    - Tent the tenderloins loosely with foil and let them rest for about 10 minutes to allow the juices to redistribute.
7. Slice and Serve:
    - Slice the smoked pork tenderloins into medallions and serve hot.

- Optionally, drizzle with any accumulated juices or a simple sauce of your choice (e.g., barbecue sauce, mustard sauce, or chimichurri).

Tips:

- Pork tenderloin is a lean cut of meat, so be careful not to overcook it to prevent dryness. Aim for an internal temperature of 145°F (63°C) for juicy and tender pork.
- Feel free to experiment with different dry rubs or seasoning blends to customize the flavor profile of the smoked pork tenderloin.
- Serve smoked pork tenderloin with your favorite sides like roasted vegetables, mashed potatoes, or a fresh salad.

Enjoy your delicious and smoky smoked pork tenderloin as a main course for a special meal or barbecue gathering. The flavorful and juicy meat will be a hit with family and friends!

Smoked Chicken Thighs

Ingredients:

- Chicken thighs, bone-in and skin-on (you can use either fresh or thawed frozen thighs)
- Olive oil
- Dry rub or seasoning blend (e.g., salt, pepper, paprika, garlic powder, onion powder, thyme, rosemary)
- Wood chips or chunks for smoking (such as applewood, hickory, cherry, or pecan)

Instructions:

1. Prep the Chicken Thighs:
   - Pat the chicken thighs dry with paper towels. Trimming excess skin and fat is optional but can help the seasonings penetrate better.
2. Season the Chicken Thighs:
   - Drizzle the chicken thighs with olive oil to help the seasoning adhere.
   - Season both sides of the thighs generously with your dry rub or seasoning blend. Ensure all surfaces are well coated.
3. Preheat the Smoker:
   - Preheat your smoker to a temperature of approximately 225-250°F (107-121°C). Use your preferred smoking wood chips or chunks to infuse flavor into the chicken (fruitwoods like apple or cherry work well).
4. Smoke the Chicken Thighs:
   - Place the seasoned chicken thighs directly on the smoker grate, skin-side up.
   - Close the lid of the smoker and let the chicken thighs smoke for about 1.5 to 2 hours, or until they reach an internal temperature of 165°F (74°C) when measured with a meat thermometer inserted into the thickest part of the meat.
5. Maintain Smoke and Temperature:
   - Monitor the temperature of your smoker throughout the smoking process. Add more wood chips or chunks as needed to maintain a steady flow of smoke.
6. Optional Finishing Touch (Crispy Skin):
   - If you prefer crispy skin, you can transfer the smoked chicken thighs to a preheated grill or oven (set to broil) for a few minutes at the end of the cooking process to crisp up the skin. Watch closely to prevent burning.
7. Rest and Serve:

- Once the chicken thighs reach the desired internal temperature, remove them from the smoker.
- Let the smoked chicken thighs rest for a few minutes before serving to allow the juices to redistribute.

8. Serve and Enjoy:
    - Serve the smoked chicken thighs hot as a main course or slice them up for use in sandwiches, salads, or other dishes.

Tips:

- For additional flavor, you can brine the chicken thighs before seasoning and smoking.
- Experiment with different dry rubs or marinades to customize the flavor of the smoked chicken thighs.
- Serve smoked chicken thighs with your favorite sides like coleslaw, baked beans, cornbread, or roasted vegetables.

Enjoy your delicious and smoky smoked chicken thighs, perfect for any barbecue or gathering. The tender and flavorful meat will be a hit with everyone at the table!

Smoked Bratwurst

Ingredients:

- Bratwurst sausages (fresh, uncooked)
- Wood chips or chunks for smoking (hickory, applewood, cherry, or another favorite smoking wood)
- Mustard, sauerkraut, buns (optional, for serving)

Instructions:

1. Prepare the Bratwurst:
    - Start with fresh, uncooked bratwurst sausages. If they are linked together, you can leave them linked or separate them into individual sausages.
2. Preheat the Smoker:
    - Preheat your smoker to a temperature of about 225-250°F (107-121°C). Use your choice of smoking wood chips or chunks for flavor. Soak wood chips in water for about 30 minutes before using, if desired.
3. Smoke the Bratwurst:
    - Place the bratwurst sausages directly on the smoker grate, leaving some space between them for the smoke to circulate.
4. Add Smoke:
    - Add the wood chips or chunks to the smoker according to the manufacturer's instructions. Close the lid of the smoker to trap the smoke inside.
5. Smoke the Bratwurst for 1-2 Hours:
    - Let the bratwurst smoke for about 1 to 2 hours, or until they reach an internal temperature of 160°F (71°C) when measured with a meat thermometer inserted into the center of the sausages.
6. Finish and Serve:
    - Once the bratwurst are fully smoked and cooked through, remove them from the smoker.
    - Optionally, you can finish the bratwurst by searing them on a hot grill or skillet for a crispy exterior.
7. Serve and Enjoy:
    - Serve the smoked bratwurst hot with your favorite condiments like mustard, sauerkraut, or in buns for delicious smoked bratwurst sandwiches.

Tips:

- To enhance the flavor, you can marinate the bratwurst in beer or a mixture of beer and onions before smoking.
- Experiment with different wood types for varying levels of smokiness. Hickory, applewood, and cherry wood are popular choices for smoking sausages.
- Use a meat thermometer to ensure the bratwurst reach a safe internal temperature of 160°F (71°C) for fully cooked sausage.

Smoked bratwurst makes a fantastic addition to any barbecue or gathering. The smoky aroma and rich flavor will be a hit with friends and family. Enjoy your homemade smoked bratwurst!

Smoked Cauliflower Steaks

Ingredients:

- 1 head of cauliflower
- Olive oil
- Salt and pepper, to taste
- Your favorite spices or seasonings (e.g., garlic powder, paprika, cumin, curry powder)
- Wood chips or chunks for smoking (such as applewood, hickory, or mesquite)

Instructions:

1. Prepare the Cauliflower:
   - Remove the outer leaves from the cauliflower and trim the stem end, leaving the core intact. Cut the cauliflower into thick slices, about 1-inch thick, to create cauliflower steaks. Try to keep the slices intact.
2. Season the Cauliflower Steaks:
   - Brush both sides of each cauliflower steak with olive oil to coat lightly.
   - Season the cauliflower steaks generously with salt, pepper, and your choice of spices or seasonings. Ensure both sides are well seasoned.
3. Preheat the Smoker:
   - Preheat your smoker to a temperature of about 225-250°F (107-121°C). Use your preferred smoking wood chips or chunks for flavor.
4. Smoke the Cauliflower Steaks:
   - Place the seasoned cauliflower steaks directly on the smoker grate.
   - Close the lid of the smoker and let the cauliflower steaks smoke for approximately 45 minutes to 1 hour, or until they are tender and have absorbed a nice smoky flavor. The exact smoking time may vary based on the thickness of the cauliflower steaks.
5. Check for Doneness:
   - Use a fork or knife to check the tenderness of the cauliflower steaks. They should be easily pierced with a fork and have a slightly caramelized exterior.
6. Serve and Enjoy:
   - Remove the smoked cauliflower steaks from the smoker and transfer them to a serving platter.
   - Serve the smoked cauliflower steaks hot as a delicious and flavorful vegetarian main course or side dish.

Tips:

- Feel free to customize the seasoning of the cauliflower steaks with your favorite spices or seasonings. Smoked paprika, garlic powder, and cumin are excellent choices for added flavor.
- For additional richness, you can sprinkle grated Parmesan cheese or drizzle balsamic glaze over the smoked cauliflower steaks before serving.
- Serve the smoked cauliflower steaks alongside a fresh salad, roasted vegetables, or a grain-based dish for a complete meal.

Smoking cauliflower steaks is a unique and delicious way to enjoy this versatile vegetable. The smoky flavor adds depth to the cauliflower's natural sweetness, creating a dish that's sure to impress!

Smoked Ratatouille

Ingredients:

- 1 eggplant, diced
- 2 zucchinis, diced
- 1 bell pepper (red, yellow, or orange), diced
- 1 onion, diced
- 2-3 tomatoes, diced
- 4 cloves garlic, minced
- Olive oil
- Salt and pepper, to taste
- Herbs de Provence (or a blend of dried herbs like thyme, rosemary, oregano)
- Wood chips or chunks for smoking (such as applewood, cherry, or hickory)

Instructions:

1. Preheat the Smoker:
    - Preheat your smoker to a temperature of about 225-250°F (107-121°C). Use your preferred smoking wood chips or chunks for flavor.
2. Prepare the Vegetables:
    - In a large bowl, combine the diced eggplant, zucchinis, bell pepper, onion, tomatoes, and minced garlic.
    - Drizzle the vegetables with olive oil and season with salt, pepper, and herbs de Provence. Toss well to coat the vegetables evenly.
3. Smoke the Vegetables:
    - Spread the seasoned vegetables evenly on a large baking sheet or shallow pan that can withstand the smoker's heat.
    - Place the pan of vegetables in the preheated smoker.
4. Smoke for 1.5-2 Hours:
    - Let the vegetables smoke for about 1.5 to 2 hours, stirring occasionally, or until they are tender and have absorbed a smoky flavor. The exact smoking time may vary based on the heat of your smoker and the desired level of smokiness.
5. Finish and Serve:
    - Once the vegetables are smoked to your liking, remove them from the smoker.
    - Transfer the smoked vegetables to a serving dish and adjust the seasoning if needed.

- Serve the smoked ratatouille hot as a side dish or as a main course with crusty bread or cooked grains.

Tips:

- Feel free to customize the vegetables used in the ratatouille based on what you have on hand or your personal preferences.
- Add extra flavor by incorporating fresh herbs like basil or parsley into the smoked ratatouille just before serving.
- Smoked ratatouille can be enjoyed warm or at room temperature, making it a versatile and delicious dish for any occasion.

Smoking ratatouille elevates this traditional vegetable medley to a whole new level of flavor. Enjoy the smoky richness of the dish as a side or main course, and savor the unique combination of smoked vegetables with Mediterranean-inspired seasonings!

Smoked Meat Tacos

Ingredients:

For the Smoked Meat:

- 1 pound (450g) of your preferred smoked meat (such as brisket, pulled pork, smoked chicken, or smoked beef)

For the Tacos:

- Corn or flour tortillas (8-10, depending on size)
- Salsa (store-bought or homemade)
- Guacamole or sliced avocado
- Chopped fresh cilantro
- Diced onions
- Lime wedges
- Optional: Shredded cheese, sour cream, hot sauce

Instructions:

1. Prepare the Smoked Meat:
   - Start by smoking your preferred meat (brisket, pulled pork, chicken, beef, etc.) until it's tender and flavorful. You can use a smoker or grill with smoking wood chips or chunks for this step. Follow the smoking instructions specific to your chosen meat.
2. Shred or Slice the Meat:
   - Once the meat is smoked and cooked to perfection, shred or slice it into bite-sized pieces. Remove any excess fat or skin as needed.
3. Warm the Tortillas:
   - Heat the corn or flour tortillas in a dry skillet or on a griddle until they are warm and lightly toasted. Keep them warm by wrapping in a clean kitchen towel or aluminum foil.
4. Assemble the Tacos:
   - Place a spoonful of the smoked meat onto each warm tortilla.
5. Add Toppings:
   - Top the smoked meat with your favorite toppings, such as salsa, guacamole or sliced avocado, chopped cilantro, diced onions, and a squeeze of lime juice.
   - Optionally, add shredded cheese, sour cream, or hot sauce for extra flavor.
6. Serve and Enjoy:

- Arrange the smoked meat tacos on a serving platter.
- Serve immediately and enjoy these delicious tacos with your favorite side dishes or accompaniments.

Tips:

- Experiment with different types of smoked meat to vary the flavor of your tacos. Brisket, pulled pork, and smoked chicken are popular choices.
- Customize the toppings based on your preferences. Additional toppings like shredded lettuce, diced tomatoes, or pickled jalapeños can also be added.
- Serve smoked meat tacos with rice and beans, Mexican street corn, or a side salad for a complete meal.

These smoked meat tacos are sure to be a hit at any gathering or taco night. Enjoy the smoky, savory goodness of the meat paired with fresh and vibrant toppings, all wrapped up in warm tortillas!

Smoked Beef Burgers

Ingredients:

- Ground beef (preferably 80% lean, 20% fat)
- Salt and pepper, to taste
- Optional seasonings (garlic powder, onion powder, paprika, etc.)
- Burger buns
- Cheese slices (optional)
- Burger toppings of your choice (lettuce, tomato, onion, pickles, etc.)
- Condiments (ketchup, mustard, mayo, barbecue sauce, etc.)
- Wood chips or chunks for smoking (hickory, mesquite, cherry, etc.)

Instructions:

1. Prepare the Smoker:
    - Preheat your smoker to a temperature of about 225-250°F (107-121°C). Use your preferred smoking wood chips or chunks to add flavor to the burgers.
2. Form the Burger Patties:
    - In a large bowl, gently mix the ground beef with salt, pepper, and any optional seasonings. Avoid over-mixing to keep the patties tender.
    - Divide the seasoned beef mixture into equal-sized portions and form them into burger patties, about 1/2 to 3/4 inch thick. Use your thumb to make a slight indentation in the center of each patty to prevent it from puffing up during cooking.
3. Smoke the Burger Patties:
    - Place the formed burger patties directly on the smoker grate, leaving some space between each patty for even smoking.
    - Close the lid of the smoker and let the burger patties smoke for approximately 1 to 1.5 hours, or until they reach an internal temperature of at least 160°F (71°C) when measured with a meat thermometer.
4. Optional: Add Cheese (if desired):
    - If you like cheeseburgers, you can add cheese slices to the smoked burger patties during the last few minutes of smoking. Close the lid to allow the cheese to melt.
5. Toast the Burger Buns (Optional):
    - While the burger patties are smoking, you can lightly toast the burger buns on the smoker or a grill for added flavor and texture.
6. Assemble the Smoked Beef Burgers:

- Once the burger patties are fully smoked and cooked through, remove them from the smoker.
- Place each smoked burger patty on a toasted bun and top with your favorite burger toppings and condiments.

7. Serve and Enjoy:
   - Serve the smoked beef burgers immediately while they are hot and juicy. Enjoy the delicious smoky flavor of these unique burgers!

Tips:

- Experiment with different wood types to customize the flavor of your smoked beef burgers. Hickory and mesquite impart a bold smoky flavor, while cherry and applewood provide a sweeter, milder smoke.
- Be sure to use a meat thermometer to ensure the burger patties reach a safe internal temperature of at least 160°F (71°C) for ground beef.
- Customize your smoked beef burgers with a variety of toppings and condiments to suit your taste preferences.

These smoked beef burgers are perfect for a barbecue or any occasion where you want to impress with delicious, flavorful burgers. Enjoy the rich smokiness and juiciness of these smoked creations!

Smoked Lobster Tails

Ingredients:

- Lobster tails (fresh or frozen, thawed)
- Butter, melted
- Garlic, minced (optional)
- Salt and pepper, to taste
- Lemon wedges, for serving
- Wood chips or chunks for smoking (such as applewood or cherry)

Instructions:

1. Prepare the Lobster Tails:
    - If using frozen lobster tails, thaw them completely in the refrigerator before cooking.
    - Using kitchen shears, carefully cut the top shell of each lobster tail lengthwise down the middle, exposing the meat. Do not cut through the underside of the tail.
2. Season the Lobster Tails:
    - Brush the exposed lobster meat with melted butter. You can also mix the melted butter with minced garlic, salt, and pepper for added flavor.
3. Preheat the Smoker:
    - Preheat your smoker to a temperature of about 225-250°F (107-121°C). Use your choice of smoking wood chips or chunks for flavor.
4. Smoke the Lobster Tails:
    - Place the prepared lobster tails directly on the smoker grate, meat side up.
    - Close the lid of the smoker and let the lobster tails smoke for approximately 30-40 minutes, or until the meat is opaque and cooked through. The internal temperature of the lobster meat should reach 135°F (57°C).
5. Serve and Enjoy:
    - Once the lobster tails are smoked and cooked, remove them from the smoker.
    - Serve the smoked lobster tails hot with lemon wedges on the side.

Tips:

- To enhance the smoky flavor, you can use wood chips or chunks like applewood or cherry, which impart a mild and sweet smoke that complements seafood well.

- Avoid overcooking the lobster tails to prevent them from becoming tough. Aim for a slightly firm texture with opaque meat.
- Serve smoked lobster tails as a main dish with sides like rice, salad, or roasted vegetables for a complete meal.

Smoking lobster tails adds a unique and delicious twist to this elegant seafood dish. Enjoy the delicate smoky flavor and tender texture of the smoked lobster tails for a special meal or celebration!

Smoked Meatballs in BBQ Sauce

Ingredients:

For the Meatballs:

- 1 pound (450g) ground beef (or a combination of ground beef and pork)
- 1/2 cup breadcrumbs
- 1/4 cup milk
- 1/4 cup grated Parmesan cheese
- 1 egg, beaten
- 2 cloves garlic, minced
- 1 teaspoon salt
- 1/2 teaspoon black pepper
- 1/2 teaspoon onion powder
- 1/2 teaspoon smoked paprika (optional)

For the BBQ Sauce:

- 1 cup barbecue sauce (your favorite store-bought or homemade)
- 2 tablespoons ketchup
- 1 tablespoon Worcestershire sauce
- 1 tablespoon brown sugar
- 1 tablespoon apple cider vinegar
- 1 teaspoon smoked paprika (optional)
- Salt and pepper, to taste

Instructions:

1. Prepare the Meatballs:
    - In a large mixing bowl, combine the breadcrumbs and milk. Let it sit for a few minutes until the breadcrumbs absorb the milk.
    - Add the ground beef, grated Parmesan cheese, beaten egg, minced garlic, salt, black pepper, onion powder, and smoked paprika to the bowl. Mix until well combined.
2. Form the Meatballs:
    - Shape the meat mixture into meatballs, about 1 to 1.5 inches in diameter. You should be able to make around 20-24 meatballs with this amount of mixture.
3. Preheat and Smoke:

- Preheat your smoker to a temperature of about 225-250°F (107-121°C). Use your preferred smoking wood chips or chunks for flavor (hickory, applewood, or cherry work well).

4. Smoke the Meatballs:
   - Place the formed meatballs directly on the smoker grate, leaving some space between each meatball for the smoke to circulate.
   - Close the lid of the smoker and let the meatballs smoke for approximately 1 to 1.5 hours, or until they are cooked through and have a nice smoky flavor. The internal temperature of the meatballs should reach at least 160°F (71°C).
5. Prepare the BBQ Sauce:
   - While the meatballs are smoking, prepare the BBQ sauce. In a small saucepan, combine the barbecue sauce, ketchup, Worcestershire sauce, brown sugar, apple cider vinegar, smoked paprika, salt, and pepper. Heat over medium heat, stirring occasionally, until the sauce is heated through and slightly thickened.
6. Glaze the Meatballs:
   - When the meatballs are almost done smoking, brush or spoon the BBQ sauce over each meatball to coat them generously.
7. Serve and Enjoy:
   - Transfer the smoked meatballs to a serving platter and serve hot, garnished with extra BBQ sauce if desired.
   - Enjoy these delicious smoked meatballs as an appetizer or main course, paired with sides like mashed potatoes, coleslaw, or a green salad.

Tips:

- You can use a combination of ground meats for the meatballs, such as beef and pork, for added flavor and juiciness.
- Customize the BBQ sauce to your taste by adjusting the sweetness, tanginess, and spiciness levels.
- If you prefer, you can also finish the smoked meatballs on a hot grill or in the oven to caramelize the BBQ sauce.

These smoked meatballs in BBQ sauce are sure to be a hit at any gathering or barbecue.

Enjoy the smoky, savory flavors and tender texture of these delicious meatballs!

Smoked Turkey Legs

Ingredients:

- Turkey legs (as many as desired)
- Olive oil or melted butter
- Salt and pepper, to taste
- Optional seasoning blend (paprika, garlic powder, onion powder, thyme, rosemary)
- Wood chips or chunks for smoking (hickory, applewood, cherry)

Instructions:

1. Prepare the Turkey Legs:
    - Rinse the turkey legs under cold water and pat them dry with paper towels.
    - Rub the turkey legs with olive oil or melted butter to help the seasonings adhere.
2. Season the Turkey Legs:
    - Season the turkey legs generously with salt, pepper, and your preferred seasoning blend. Make sure to coat all sides of the turkey legs evenly.
3. Preheat the Smoker:
    - Preheat your smoker to a temperature of about 225-250°F (107-121°C). Use your choice of smoking wood chips or chunks for flavor.
4. Smoke the Turkey Legs:
    - Place the seasoned turkey legs directly on the smoker grate, making sure they are not touching each other for even smoking.
    - Close the lid of the smoker and let the turkey legs smoke for approximately 3-4 hours, or until they reach an internal temperature of at least 165°F (74°C) when measured with a meat thermometer inserted into the thickest part of the meat.
5. Monitor the Smoking Process:
    - Keep an eye on the smoker temperature throughout the smoking process. Add more wood chips or chunks as needed to maintain a steady flow of smoke.
6. Rest and Serve:
    - Once the turkey legs reach the desired internal temperature and are nicely smoked, remove them from the smoker.
    - Let the smoked turkey legs rest for a few minutes before serving to allow the juices to redistribute.
7. Serve and Enjoy:

- Serve the smoked turkey legs hot as a main course. They pair well with classic sides like mashed potatoes, stuffing, cranberry sauce, or green beans.

Tips:

- For extra flavor, you can brine the turkey legs before smoking. A simple brine of salt, sugar, and herbs dissolved in water can enhance the juiciness and flavor of the turkey.
- Experiment with different seasoning blends or marinades to customize the flavor of the smoked turkey legs.
- Consider using a drip pan underneath the turkey legs in the smoker to catch any drippings and prevent flare-ups.

Smoking turkey legs is a great way to enjoy delicious smoked turkey with a beautiful smoky flavor. Whether for a holiday meal or a backyard barbecue, smoked turkey legs are sure to be a hit with family and friends!

Smoked Chili

Ingredients:

- 1 pound (450g) smoked meat, such as smoked brisket, smoked pork shoulder (pulled pork), or smoked sausage, diced
- 1 onion, diced
- 3 cloves garlic, minced
- 1 bell pepper, diced (any color)
- 1 jalapeño pepper, seeded and diced (optional, for heat)
- 1 can (15 oz) diced tomatoes
- 1 can (15 oz) kidney beans, drained and rinsed
- 1 can (15 oz) black beans, drained and rinsed
- 2 tablespoons tomato paste
- 2 cups beef or chicken broth
- 2 tablespoons chili powder
- 1 tablespoon smoked paprika
- 1 teaspoon ground cumin
- 1 teaspoon dried oregano
- Salt and pepper, to taste
- Olive oil, for cooking
- Optional toppings: shredded cheese, sour cream, sliced green onions, chopped cilantro, diced avocado

Instructions:

1. Prepare the Smoked Meat:
    - If you haven't already smoked your meat, prepare it by smoking a brisket, pork shoulder, or sausage until tender and flavorful. Dice the smoked meat into bite-sized pieces.
2. Sauté the Vegetables:
    - Heat a large pot or Dutch oven over medium heat. Add a drizzle of olive oil.
    - Add the diced onion, garlic, bell pepper, and jalapeño (if using). Sauté for 5-7 minutes, or until the vegetables are softened.
3. Add Tomatoes and Beans:
    - Stir in the diced tomatoes, kidney beans, black beans, and tomato paste.
    - Pour in the beef or chicken broth to loosen the mixture.
4. Season the Chili:
    - Add the chili powder, smoked paprika, ground cumin, dried oregano, salt, and pepper to the pot. Stir well to combine.

5. Simmer the Chili:
    - Bring the chili to a simmer over medium-low heat. Cover the pot and let it simmer for at least 30 minutes to allow the flavors to meld together. Stir occasionally.
6. Adjust Seasoning:
    - Taste the chili and adjust the seasoning as needed with more salt, pepper, or spices according to your preference.
7. Serve the Smoked Chili:
    - Ladle the smoked chili into bowls.
    - Garnish each bowl of chili with diced smoked meat and your choice of optional toppings such as shredded cheese, sour cream, sliced green onions, chopped cilantro, or diced avocado.
8. Enjoy:
    - Serve the smoked chili hot and enjoy the delicious smoky flavors!

Tips:

- Feel free to customize this smoked chili recipe with your favorite smoked meats and additional vegetables.
- If you prefer a thicker chili, you can blend a portion of the chili mixture using an immersion blender or food processor, then stir it back into the pot.
- Store any leftovers in the refrigerator for up to 3-4 days or freeze for longer storage. The flavors will continue to develop over time.

Smoked chili is perfect for cozy dinners and gatherings. The combination of smoky meats, spices, and beans creates a satisfying and comforting dish that's sure to be a hit!

Smoked Garlic Butter Shrimp

Ingredients:

- 1 pound (450g) large shrimp, peeled and deveined
- 4 tablespoons unsalted butter
- 4 cloves garlic, minced
- 1 tablespoon lemon juice
- 1 teaspoon smoked paprika
- Salt and pepper, to taste
- Fresh parsley, chopped (for garnish)
- Wood chips or chunks for smoking (such as applewood or hickory)

Instructions:

1. Prepare the Smoker:
   - Preheat your smoker to a temperature of about 225-250°F (107-121°C). Use your preferred smoking wood chips or chunks for flavor.
2. Prepare the Shrimp:
   - Rinse the shrimp under cold water and pat them dry with paper towels.
   - In a bowl, combine the shrimp with smoked paprika, salt, and pepper. Toss to coat the shrimp evenly.
3. Make the Garlic Butter Sauce:
   - In a small saucepan or microwave-safe bowl, melt the butter over low heat.
   - Add the minced garlic to the melted butter and cook gently for 1-2 minutes, stirring occasionally, until the garlic is fragrant but not browned.
   - Remove the garlic butter from the heat and stir in the lemon juice. Set aside.
4. Smoke the Shrimp:
   - Arrange the seasoned shrimp in a single layer on a perforated grill tray or aluminum foil pan that can withstand the heat of the smoker.
   - Place the shrimp in the preheated smoker.
5. Smoke for 20-30 Minutes:
   - Smoke the shrimp for about 20-30 minutes, or until they are opaque and cooked through. The exact smoking time may vary based on the size of the shrimp and the heat of your smoker.
6. Toss with Garlic Butter Sauce:
   - Once the shrimp are smoked and cooked, transfer them to a large bowl.

- Pour the garlic butter sauce over the smoked shrimp and toss gently to coat the shrimp with the sauce.
7. Serve and Garnish:
    - Transfer the smoked garlic butter shrimp to a serving platter.
    - Garnish with chopped fresh parsley.
    - Serve the smoked garlic butter shrimp hot as an appetizer or main course.

Tips:

- Use fresh, high-quality shrimp for the best flavor and texture.
- Feel free to adjust the amount of garlic, butter, lemon juice, and spices according to your taste preferences.
- Serve the smoked garlic butter shrimp with crusty bread, rice, or pasta to soak up the delicious sauce.

Smoked garlic butter shrimp is a delightful dish that's perfect for any occasion. The smoky flavor pairs beautifully with the buttery garlic sauce, creating a memorable seafood experience. Enjoy this dish with friends and family!

Smoked Asparagus

Ingredients:

- Fresh asparagus spears, woody ends trimmed
- Olive oil
- Salt and pepper, to taste
- Optional seasonings (garlic powder, lemon zest, smoked paprika)
- Wood chips or chunks for smoking (such as applewood or hickory)

Instructions:

1. Preheat the Smoker:
    - Preheat your smoker to a temperature of about 225-250°F (107-121°C). Use your preferred smoking wood chips or chunks for flavor.
2. Prepare the Asparagus:
    - Rinse the asparagus spears under cold water and pat them dry with paper towels.
    - Place the asparagus spears in a large bowl and drizzle with olive oil. Toss to coat the asparagus evenly.
3. Season the Asparagus:
    - Season the asparagus with salt, pepper, and any optional seasonings of your choice, such as garlic powder, lemon zest, or smoked paprika. Toss to coat.
4. Smoke the Asparagus:
    - Arrange the seasoned asparagus spears on a perforated grill tray or aluminum foil pan that can withstand the heat of the smoker.
    - Place the tray of asparagus in the preheated smoker.
5. Smoke for 20-30 Minutes:
    - Smoke the asparagus for about 20-30 minutes, or until the spears are tender and lightly charred, with a slight smoky flavor. The exact smoking time may vary based on the thickness of the asparagus and the heat of your smoker.
6. Serve and Enjoy:
    - Remove the smoked asparagus from the smoker and transfer to a serving platter.
    - Serve the smoked asparagus hot as a side dish or appetizer.

Tips:

- Choose fresh and firm asparagus spears for the best results.
- Avoid overcooking the asparagus to retain its crisp texture.
- Experiment with different seasonings to customize the flavor of the smoked asparagus.
- Serve smoked asparagus with a squeeze of fresh lemon juice or a sprinkle of grated Parmesan cheese for added flavor.

Smoked asparagus is a delicious and healthy side dish that pairs well with grilled meats, seafood, or pasta. Enjoy the unique smoky flavor of the asparagus, which adds a special touch to any meal!

Smoked Beef Kabobs

Ingredients:

- 1.5 pounds (680g) beef sirloin or beef tenderloin, cut into 1-inch cubes
- Assorted vegetables for kabobs (bell peppers, onions, cherry tomatoes, mushrooms, zucchini, etc.)
- Wooden or metal skewers, soaked in water (if using wooden skewers)
- Olive oil, for brushing

For the Marinade:

- 1/4 cup soy sauce
- 1/4 cup olive oil
- 2 tablespoons Worcestershire sauce
- 2 tablespoons balsamic vinegar
- 2 cloves garlic, minced
- 1 teaspoon smoked paprika
- 1 teaspoon dried thyme
- Salt and pepper, to taste

Instructions:

1. Prepare the Marinade:
   - In a bowl, whisk together all the marinade ingredients: soy sauce, olive oil, Worcestershire sauce, balsamic vinegar, minced garlic, smoked paprika, dried thyme, salt, and pepper.
2. Marinate the Beef:
   - Place the beef cubes in a resealable plastic bag or a bowl. Pour the marinade over the beef, ensuring all pieces are coated. Marinate in the refrigerator for at least 1 hour, or ideally overnight for maximum flavor.
3. Prepare the Vegetables:
   - Cut the vegetables into bite-sized pieces suitable for skewering. Bell peppers, onions, cherry tomatoes, mushrooms, and zucchini work well for kabobs.
4. Assemble the Kabobs:
   - Preheat your smoker to a temperature of about 225-250°F (107-121°C) using your preferred smoking wood chips or chunks.
   - Thread the marinated beef cubes and assorted vegetables onto the skewers, alternating between meat and vegetables.
5. Smoke the Kabobs:

- Place the assembled kabobs on the smoker grate, leaving space between each skewer for the smoke to circulate.
- Close the lid of the smoker and smoke the kabobs for approximately 1 to 1.5 hours, or until the beef is cooked to your desired doneness and the vegetables are tender.

6. Brush with Olive Oil:
   - About halfway through the smoking process, brush the kabobs with olive oil to keep them moist and enhance the flavor.
7. Serve and Enjoy:
   - Remove the smoked beef kabobs from the smoker.
   - Serve the kabobs hot with a side of rice, salad, or crusty bread.
   - Enjoy the delicious, smoky flavor of these beef kabobs straight from the smoker!

Tips:

- Choose tender cuts of beef like sirloin or tenderloin for juicy and flavorful kabobs.
- Soak wooden skewers in water for at least 30 minutes before using to prevent them from burning in the smoker.
- Feel free to customize the vegetables based on your preferences or what's in season.
- Serve smoked beef kabobs with your favorite dipping sauce or additional marinade on the side for extra flavor.

Smoked beef kabobs are perfect for outdoor gatherings or weeknight dinners. The marinade infuses the beef with savory flavors, and the smoking process adds a delightful smoky aroma. Enjoy making and savoring these delicious kabobs!

Smoked Beef Brisket Chili

Ingredients:

- 2 pounds (about 900g) smoked beef brisket, chopped into bite-sized pieces
- 1 onion, diced
- 3 cloves garlic, minced
- 1 bell pepper, diced
- 1 jalapeño pepper, seeded and diced (optional, for heat)
- 1 can (15 oz) diced tomatoes
- 1 can (15 oz) kidney beans, drained and rinsed
- 1 can (15 oz) black beans, drained and rinsed
- 2 cups beef broth
- 2 tablespoons tomato paste
- 2 tablespoons chili powder
- 1 tablespoon smoked paprika
- 1 teaspoon ground cumin
- Salt and pepper, to taste
- Olive oil, for cooking
- Optional toppings: shredded cheese, sour cream, sliced green onions, chopped cilantro

Instructions:

1. Sauté the Vegetables:
   - Heat a large pot or Dutch oven over medium heat. Add a drizzle of olive oil.
   - Add the diced onion, garlic, bell pepper, and jalapeño (if using). Sauté for 5-7 minutes, or until the vegetables are softened.
2. Add Brisket and Tomatoes:
   - Add the chopped smoked beef brisket to the pot with the sautéed vegetables.
   - Pour in the diced tomatoes (including juices) and beef broth.
3. Season the Chili:
   - Stir in the tomato paste, chili powder, smoked paprika, ground cumin, salt, and pepper.
   - Mix well to combine all ingredients.
4. Simmer the Chili:
   - Bring the chili to a simmer over medium-low heat.
   - Cover the pot and let the chili simmer for at least 30 minutes to allow the flavors to meld together. Stir occasionally.

5. Adjust Seasoning:
    - Taste the chili and adjust the seasoning as needed with more salt, pepper, or spices according to your preference.
6. Serve the Chili:
    - Ladle the smoked beef brisket chili into bowls.
    - Garnish each bowl of chili with optional toppings such as shredded cheese, sour cream, sliced green onions, or chopped cilantro.
7. Enjoy:
    - Serve the smoked beef brisket chili hot and enjoy the rich, smoky flavors!

Tips:

- Use leftover smoked beef brisket for this recipe, or smoke a brisket specifically for making chili.
- Feel free to add additional vegetables like corn or diced carrots to the chili for extra flavor and texture.
- Adjust the level of spiciness by adding more or less chili powder and jalapeño peppers.
- Serve the smoked beef brisket chili with cornbread, rice, or tortilla chips for a complete meal.

Smoked beef brisket chili is a comforting and satisfying dish that's perfect for cold weather or game day gatherings. The tender chunks of smoked brisket add a unique smoky flavor to this classic chili recipe. Enjoy making and sharing this delicious chili with family and friends!

Smoked Stuffed Pork Loin

Ingredients:

- 1 pork loin roast (about 3-4 pounds)
- Salt and pepper, to taste
- 2 tablespoons olive oil

For the Stuffing:

- 1 cup breadcrumbs
- 1/2 cup finely chopped onion
- 1/2 cup finely chopped celery
- 1/2 cup finely chopped mushrooms
- 2 cloves garlic, minced
- 2 tablespoons butter
- 1/2 teaspoon dried thyme
- 1/2 teaspoon dried sage
- Salt and pepper, to taste
- 1/2 cup chicken or vegetable broth (as needed to moisten)

Instructions:

1. Prepare the Pork Loin:
    - Preheat your smoker to a temperature of about 225-250°F (107-121°C). Use your preferred smoking wood chips or chunks for flavor (applewood or hickory work well).
    - Trim any excess fat from the pork loin. Butterfly the pork loin by cutting it lengthwise almost all the way through, then open it like a book.
2. Make the Stuffing:
    - In a skillet, melt the butter over medium heat. Add the chopped onion, celery, and mushrooms. Sauté until the vegetables are softened.
    - Add the minced garlic, dried thyme, dried sage, salt, and pepper to the skillet. Cook for another minute.
    - Remove the skillet from the heat and stir in the breadcrumbs. Gradually add chicken or vegetable broth as needed to moisten the stuffing mixture. The stuffing should hold together but not be too wet.
3. Fill and Roll the Pork Loin:
    - Season the inside of the butterflied pork loin with salt and pepper.
    - Spread the stuffing evenly over the inside of the pork loin.

- Carefully roll up the pork loin with the stuffing inside and tie it securely with kitchen twine at regular intervals to hold its shape.
4. Season and Smoke the Pork Loin:
    - Rub the outside of the pork loin with olive oil and season generously with salt and pepper.
    - Place the stuffed and tied pork loin on the smoker grate.
5. Smoke the Pork Loin:
    - Place the pork loin in the preheated smoker.
    - Close the lid of the smoker and smoke the pork loin for approximately 2.5 to 3 hours, or until the internal temperature reaches 145°F (63°C) when measured with a meat thermometer inserted into the thickest part of the meat.
6. Rest and Serve:
    - Once the smoked stuffed pork loin is cooked, remove it from the smoker and let it rest for about 10-15 minutes before slicing.
    - Remove the kitchen twine and slice the smoked stuffed pork loin into thick slices.
7. Serve and Enjoy:
    - Serve the smoked stuffed pork loin slices hot, accompanied by your favorite side dishes such as roasted vegetables, mashed potatoes, or a green salad.

Tips:

- Customize the stuffing with your favorite ingredients such as dried fruits, nuts, or fresh herbs.
- Ensure the pork loin is cooked to a safe internal temperature of 145°F (63°C) for best results.
- Use a meat thermometer to monitor the internal temperature of the pork loin during smoking.
- Leftover smoked stuffed pork loin can be refrigerated and enjoyed as delicious cold cuts for sandwiches.

Smoked stuffed pork loin makes an impressive and flavorful main dish for special occasions or family gatherings. The combination of juicy pork and savory stuffing, infused with smoky goodness, is sure to be a hit!

Smoked Buffalo Wings

Ingredients:

- 2-3 pounds of chicken wings, separated into drumettes and flats
- Olive oil
- Salt and pepper, to taste
- Buffalo sauce (store-bought or homemade)
- Butter, melted (for tossing with buffalo sauce)
- Optional: blue cheese dressing or ranch dressing, celery sticks

Instructions:

1. Prepare the Chicken Wings:
    - Rinse the chicken wings under cold water and pat them dry with paper towels.
    - Place the wings in a large bowl and drizzle with olive oil. Season with salt and pepper, tossing to coat evenly.
2. Preheat the Smoker:
    - Preheat your smoker to a temperature of about 225-250°F (107-121°C). Use your preferred smoking wood chips or chunks for flavor (hickory, applewood, or cherry work well).
3. Smoke the Chicken Wings:
    - Arrange the seasoned chicken wings on the smoker grate, making sure they are not touching each other for even smoking.
    - Close the lid of the smoker and let the wings smoke for about 1.5 to 2 hours, or until they are cooked through and have a nice smoky flavor. The internal temperature of the wings should reach at least 165°F (74°C) when measured with a meat thermometer.
4. Prepare the Buffalo Sauce:
    - In a bowl, combine the buffalo sauce and melted butter. Adjust the ratio of sauce to butter based on your desired level of heat and richness.
5. Toss the Wings in Buffalo Sauce:
    - Once the chicken wings are smoked and cooked, transfer them to a large bowl.
    - Pour the buffalo sauce mixture over the smoked wings and toss until the wings are evenly coated.
6. Serve and Enjoy:
    - Transfer the smoked buffalo wings to a serving platter.

- Serve the wings hot with blue cheese dressing or ranch dressing on the side, along with celery sticks for a classic buffalo wings experience.

Tips:

- You can adjust the smoking time based on the size of your chicken wings and the desired level of smokiness.
- For crispier wings, you can finish the smoked wings on a hot grill or in the oven after tossing them in the buffalo sauce.
- Customize the buffalo sauce by adding additional spices or hot sauce to suit your taste preferences.
- Serve smoked buffalo wings as a crowd-pleasing appetizer for game day parties, barbecues, or casual gatherings.

Smoked buffalo wings are a fantastic way to enjoy tender, flavorful chicken with a kick of buffalo sauce and smoky goodness. Whether as an appetizer or main dish, these wings are sure to be a hit at any occasion!

Smoked Cornbread

Ingredients:

- 1 cup yellow cornmeal
- 1 cup all-purpose flour
- 1 tablespoon baking powder
- 1/2 teaspoon baking soda
- 1 teaspoon salt
- 2 tablespoons granulated sugar (optional, for a sweeter cornbread)
- 1 cup buttermilk (or substitute with regular milk)
- 2 eggs
- 1/4 cup unsalted butter, melted
- Olive oil or cooking spray, for greasing
- Wood chips or chunks for smoking (such as hickory or applewood)

Instructions:

1. Preheat the Smoker:
    - Preheat your smoker to a temperature of about 225-250°F (107-121°C). Use your preferred smoking wood chips or chunks for flavor.
2. Prepare the Cornbread Batter:
    - In a large bowl, whisk together the cornmeal, flour, baking powder, baking soda, salt, and sugar (if using).
    - In another bowl, whisk together the buttermilk, eggs, and melted butter.
3. Combine Wet and Dry Ingredients:
    - Pour the wet ingredients into the dry ingredients and stir until just combined. Do not overmix.
4. Grease the Baking Dish:
    - Grease a cast iron skillet or baking dish with olive oil or cooking spray.
5. Smoke the Cornbread:
    - Pour the cornbread batter into the greased skillet or baking dish.
    - Place the skillet or baking dish in the preheated smoker.
6. Smoke for 30-40 Minutes:
    - Smoke the cornbread for about 30-40 minutes, or until the top is golden brown and a toothpick inserted into the center comes out clean.
7. Rest and Serve:
    - Remove the smoked cornbread from the smoker and let it rest in the skillet or baking dish for a few minutes.
    - Slice and serve the smoked cornbread warm.

Tips:

- You can add extra flavor to the smoked cornbread by mixing in ingredients like cooked and crumbled bacon, diced jalapeños, shredded cheese, or corn kernels into the batter before smoking.
- Serve smoked cornbread alongside barbecue meats, chili, soups, or stews for a delicious and comforting meal.
- Leftover smoked cornbread can be wrapped tightly and stored at room temperature for a day or two, or refrigerated for longer storage.

Smoked cornbread is a wonderful twist on a classic favorite, adding a subtle smoky element that elevates the dish. Enjoy the rich flavors and tender texture of smoked cornbread with your favorite meals!

Smoked Crab Legs

Ingredients:

- Crab legs (snow crab or king crab)
- Butter, melted (for serving)
- Lemon wedges (for serving)
- Old Bay seasoning or seafood seasoning (optional, for seasoning)

Instructions:

1. Preheat the Smoker:
    - Preheat your smoker to a temperature of about 225-250°F (107-121°C). Use a mild smoking wood like applewood or cherry for a gentle smoke flavor.
2. Prepare the Crab Legs:
    - Thaw the crab legs if frozen, and rinse them under cold water.
    - Use kitchen shears or a sharp knife to split the shells of the crab legs lengthwise to allow the smoke to penetrate.
3. Smoke the Crab Legs:
    - Place the split crab legs directly on the smoker grate, ensuring they are not overlapping for even smoking.
    - Close the lid of the smoker and smoke the crab legs for about 20-30 minutes. The crab legs are already cooked, so you're essentially heating them and infusing them with smoky flavor.
4. Serve the Smoked Crab Legs:
    - Remove the smoked crab legs from the smoker.
    - Serve the smoked crab legs hot with melted butter for dipping and lemon wedges on the side.
    - Optionally, sprinkle Old Bay seasoning or seafood seasoning over the crab legs for added flavor.
5. Enjoy:
    - Crack open the crab legs and enjoy the tender, smoky meat dipped in butter and a squeeze of fresh lemon.

Tips:

- Be careful not to overcook the crab legs in the smoker, as they are already cooked and simply need to be heated through.

- You can customize the seasoning by using your favorite seafood seasoning blend or simply enjoy the natural flavor of the smoked crab legs with butter and lemon.
- Serve smoked crab legs as a delicious appetizer or part of a seafood feast.

Smoking crab legs adds a delightful twist to this seafood delicacy, making them even more special and flavorful. Enjoy the unique smoky taste of smoked crab legs with family and friends!

Smoked Meat Pies

Ingredients:

For the Filling:

- 1 pound (450g) smoked meat (such as smoked brisket, smoked sausage, or smoked turkey), diced
- 1 onion, finely chopped
- 2 cloves garlic, minced
- 1 bell pepper, finely chopped
- 1 tablespoon vegetable oil
- Salt and pepper, to taste
- 1 teaspoon smoked paprika
- 1 teaspoon dried thyme
- 1/2 cup chicken or beef broth
- Optional: diced potatoes, carrots, or peas

For the Pastry:

- 2 cups all-purpose flour
- 1/2 teaspoon salt
- 1/2 cup cold unsalted butter, diced
- 1/2 cup cold water

Instructions:

1. Prepare the Filling:
    - In a skillet or frying pan, heat the vegetable oil over medium heat.
    - Add the chopped onion, garlic, and bell pepper. Sauté until softened, about 5-7 minutes.
2. Add Smoked Meat and Seasonings:
    - Add the diced smoked meat to the skillet with the sautéed vegetables.
    - Season with salt, pepper, smoked paprika, and dried thyme. Stir to combine.
3. Cook the Filling:
    - Pour in the chicken or beef broth and bring to a simmer.
    - If using diced potatoes, carrots, or peas, add them to the skillet.
    - Simmer the filling for about 10-15 minutes, or until the vegetables are tender and the liquid is reduced. Remove from heat and let the filling cool slightly.

4. Prepare the Pastry:
   - In a large bowl, combine the flour and salt.
   - Add the cold diced butter to the flour mixture. Use a pastry cutter or fork to cut the butter into the flour until the mixture resembles coarse crumbs.
5. Form the Dough:
   - Gradually add cold water to the flour mixture, mixing until the dough comes together and forms a ball.
   - Divide the dough into two portions (one slightly larger for the bottom crust and one smaller for the top crust).
6. Assemble the Pies:
   - Roll out the larger portion of dough on a lightly floured surface to about 1/8-inch thickness.
   - Use the rolled-out dough to line greased pie dishes or individual pie molds.
7. Fill and Seal the Pies:
   - Spoon the cooled smoked meat filling into the prepared pie crusts.
   - Roll out the smaller portion of dough and use it to cover the pies. Trim any excess dough and crimp the edges to seal the pies.
8. Bake the Pies:
   - Preheat your oven to 375°F (190°C).
   - Place the assembled pies on a baking sheet and bake for 25-30 minutes, or until the pastry is golden brown and cooked through.
9. Serve and Enjoy:
   - Remove the smoked meat pies from the oven and let them cool slightly before serving.
   - Enjoy the delicious smoked meat pies warm as a main course or snack.

Tips:

- Feel free to use your favorite smoked meat for the filling, such as leftover smoked brisket, smoked sausage, or smoked turkey.
- Add extra vegetables to the filling for added texture and flavor.
- Serve smoked meat pies with a side salad or pickles for a complete meal.

These smoked meat pies are a comforting and satisfying dish that's perfect for any occasion. The combination of smoky meat filling and flaky pastry crust is sure to be a hit with family and friends!

Smoked Eggplant Dip

Ingredients:

- 2 medium-sized eggplants
- 2 cloves garlic, minced
- Juice of 1 lemon
- 2 tablespoons tahini (sesame paste)
- 2 tablespoons extra-virgin olive oil
- Salt, to taste
- Pepper, to taste
- Optional garnish: chopped fresh parsley, paprika, or additional olive oil

Instructions:

1. Preheat the Smoker:
    - Preheat your smoker to a temperature of about 350°F (175°C), using your preferred smoking wood chips or chunks. Aim for a medium-high heat for roasting the eggplants.
2. Prepare the Eggplants:
    - Rinse the eggplants and pat them dry with paper towels.
    - Use a fork to poke several holes all over each eggplant to allow steam to escape during smoking.
3. Smoke the Eggplants:
    - Place the eggplants directly on the smoker grate.
    - Close the lid of the smoker and smoke the eggplants for about 30-40 minutes, or until the skin is charred and the flesh is soft and tender.
4. Cool and Peel the Eggplants:
    - Remove the smoked eggplants from the smoker and let them cool slightly.
    - Once cool enough to handle, carefully peel off the charred skin from the eggplants. Discard the skin and place the smoked eggplant flesh in a bowl.
5. Prepare the Dip:
    - Mash the smoked eggplant flesh with a fork or potato masher until smooth and creamy.
    - Add minced garlic, lemon juice, tahini, and extra-virgin olive oil to the mashed eggplant.
    - Season with salt and pepper, to taste. Mix well to combine all ingredients.
6. Adjust Seasoning:

- Taste the smoked eggplant dip and adjust the seasoning, adding more lemon juice, tahini, olive oil, or salt as needed to achieve the desired flavor and consistency.

7. Serve the Smoked Eggplant Dip:
    - Transfer the smoked eggplant dip to a serving bowl.
    - Drizzle with additional olive oil and sprinkle with chopped fresh parsley or paprika for garnish, if desired.
8. Enjoy:
    - Serve the smoked eggplant dip with pita bread, crackers, or fresh vegetables for dipping.
    - Store any leftover dip in an airtight container in the refrigerator for up to 3-4 days.

Tips:

- You can also roast the eggplants in the oven at 400°F (200°C) if you don't have a smoker. Place them on a baking sheet and roast for about 40-45 minutes until tender.
- Adjust the amount of garlic and tahini according to your taste preferences.
- For a smokier flavor, you can use a blend of different smoking woods like hickory or mesquite.

Smoked eggplant dip (baba ganoush) is a wonderful appetizer or side dish that's perfect for parties, gatherings, or simply as a tasty snack. Enjoy the smoky, creamy goodness of this flavorful dip!

Smoked Beef Wellington

Ingredients:

- 1 whole beef tenderloin (about 3-4 pounds), trimmed
- Salt and pepper, to taste
- Olive oil
- Dijon mustard
- 1 package of puff pastry (enough to wrap the beef)
- 8-10 slices of prosciutto or Parma ham
- 1 pound of mushroom duxelles (finely chopped mushrooms cooked with shallots, garlic, and herbs)
- 2-3 tablespoons butter
- 2 tablespoons chopped fresh thyme
- 1 egg, beaten (for egg wash)

Instructions:

1. Prepare the Beef:
    - Preheat your smoker to a temperature of about 225-250°F (107-121°C) using your preferred smoking wood chips or chunks (e.g., hickory, oak, or mesquite).
    - Season the beef tenderloin generously with salt and pepper.
    - Rub the tenderloin with olive oil and a thin layer of Dijon mustard.
2. Smoke the Beef Tenderloin:
    - Place the seasoned beef tenderloin directly on the smoker grate.
    - Close the lid of the smoker and smoke the tenderloin for about 1.5 to 2 hours, or until it reaches an internal temperature of 125-130°F (52-54°C) for medium-rare.
3. Prepare the Mushroom Duxelles:
    - While the beef is smoking, prepare the mushroom duxelles. Heat butter in a skillet over medium heat.
    - Add finely chopped mushrooms, shallots, and garlic to the skillet. Cook until the mushrooms release their moisture and the mixture becomes dry.
    - Season with salt, pepper, and chopped fresh thyme. Remove from heat and let cool.
4. Assemble the Beef Wellington:
    - Lay out a large sheet of plastic wrap and arrange the slices of prosciutto or Parma ham in a slightly overlapping layer.
    - Spread the mushroom duxelles evenly over the prosciutto.

- Place the smoked beef tenderloin on top of the mushroom layer.
5. Wrap with Puff Pastry:
    - Roll out the puff pastry on a lightly floured surface to a rectangle large enough to encase the beef tenderloin.
    - Place the prosciutto-covered beef tenderloin in the center of the puff pastry.
    - Use the plastic wrap to help tightly wrap the puff pastry around the beef, ensuring the seam is on the bottom.
6. Chill and Brush with Egg Wash:
    - Chill the wrapped Beef Wellington in the refrigerator for at least 30 minutes to firm up.
    - Preheat your oven to 400°F (200°C).
    - Brush the chilled Beef Wellington with beaten egg for a golden finish.
7. Bake the Beef Wellington:
    - Transfer the Beef Wellington to a baking sheet lined with parchment paper.
    - Bake in the preheated oven for 25-30 minutes, or until the puff pastry is golden brown and the internal temperature of the beef reaches 135-140°F (57-60°C) for medium-rare.
8. Rest and Serve:
    - Remove the Beef Wellington from the oven and let it rest for 10-15 minutes before slicing.
    - Slice the Beef Wellington into thick portions and serve immediately.

Tips:

- Ensure the puff pastry is rolled out thinly enough to fully cook and become crispy during baking.
- You can prepare the mushroom duxelles and wrap the Beef Wellington ahead of time, keeping it refrigerated until ready to bake.
- Serve the smoked Beef Wellington with a side of roasted vegetables, mashed potatoes, or a green salad for a complete meal.

Smoked Beef Wellington is a show-stopping dish that's perfect for special occasions and holiday dinners. The combination of tender smoked beef, savory mushroom duxelles, and flaky puff pastry is sure to impress your guests!

Smoked Ham

Ingredients:

- 1 bone-in ham (pre-cooked, about 8-10 pounds)
- Your favorite dry rub or seasoning blend
- Optional glaze ingredients (such as honey, brown sugar, mustard, maple syrup)

Instructions:

1. Prep the Ham:
    - Start with a pre-cooked bone-in ham, which can be either fully cooked or partially cooked. Ensure the ham is fully thawed if previously frozen.
2. Score the Ham:
    - Use a sharp knife to score the surface of the ham in a diamond pattern. This helps the flavors penetrate and the glaze to adhere better.
3. Apply Seasoning:
    - Generously apply your favorite dry rub or seasoning blend all over the surface of the ham. Make sure to rub it into the scored areas for maximum flavor.
4. Preheat the Smoker:
    - Preheat your smoker to a temperature of about 225-250°F (107-121°C). Use your preferred smoking wood chips or chunks. Hickory, applewood, or cherry wood are great options for smoking ham.
5. Smoke the Ham:
    - Place the seasoned ham directly on the smoker grate, flat side down.
    - Close the lid of the smoker and smoke the ham for approximately 3-4 hours, or until the internal temperature reaches about 140°F (60°C). This allows time for the smoke flavor to infuse into the ham.
6. Apply Glaze (Optional):
    - If desired, prepare a glaze using ingredients such as honey, brown sugar, mustard, or maple syrup.
    - Brush the glaze over the smoked ham during the last hour of smoking, allowing it to caramelize and create a flavorful crust.
7. Rest and Serve:
    - Once the ham reaches the desired internal temperature and is nicely smoked and glazed, remove it from the smoker.
    - Let the smoked ham rest for about 15-20 minutes before slicing to allow the juices to redistribute.
8. Slice and Enjoy:

- Slice the smoked ham and serve it warm. It pairs beautifully with sides like mashed potatoes, green beans, or a fresh salad.

Tips:

- Use a meat thermometer to monitor the internal temperature of the ham. Aim for 140°F (60°C) for fully cooked ham or 145°F (63°C) for partially cooked ham.
- Feel free to customize the seasoning and glaze according to your taste preferences. The sweetness of the glaze complements the smoky flavor of the ham.
- Leftover smoked ham can be stored in the refrigerator and used in sandwiches, soups, or other recipes.

Smoking a ham adds depth of flavor and creates a memorable dish that will be a hit at any gathering. Enjoy the rich smokiness and tender texture of smoked ham with family and friends!

Smoked Pastrami

Ingredients:

- 1 whole beef brisket (about 10-12 pounds)
- For the Cure:
    - 1 gallon water
    - 1 cup kosher salt
    - 1 cup brown sugar
    - 1/2 cup pickling spice
    - 5 cloves garlic, minced
- For the Rub:
    - 2 tablespoons coarsely ground black pepper
    - 2 tablespoons coriander seeds, toasted and coarsely ground
    - 1 tablespoon paprika
    - 1 tablespoon brown sugar
    - 1 teaspoon garlic powder
- Mustard (for slathering before smoking)

Instructions:

1. Prepare the Cure:
    - In a large pot, combine water, kosher salt, brown sugar, pickling spice, and minced garlic.
    - Bring the mixture to a boil, stirring until the salt and sugar are fully dissolved.
    - Remove from heat and let the brine cool completely.
2. Brine the Brisket:
    - Place the brisket in a large container or food-safe plastic bag.
    - Pour the cooled brine over the brisket, ensuring it is fully submerged.
    - Refrigerate and let the brisket brine for 5-7 days, flipping it once or twice a day to evenly distribute the cure.
3. Prepare the Smoker:
    - Preheat your smoker to a temperature of about 225-250°F (107-121°C). Use hardwood chips or chunks like hickory, oak, or maple for smoking.
4. Rinse and Dry the Brisket:
    - After brining, remove the brisket from the brine and rinse it thoroughly under cold water.
    - Pat the brisket dry with paper towels.
5. Apply the Rub:

- In a bowl, mix together the coarsely ground black pepper, toasted ground coriander seeds, paprika, brown sugar, and garlic powder to create the rub.
- Slather the brisket with mustard to help the rub adhere, then generously coat the brisket with the spice rub, pressing it into the meat.

6. Smoke the Pastrami:
   - Place the seasoned brisket in the preheated smoker.
   - Close the lid and smoke the brisket for about 6-8 hours, or until the internal temperature reaches 195-203°F (90-95°C) and the meat is tender and fully cooked.

7. Rest and Slice:
   - Remove the smoked pastrami from the smoker and let it rest for at least 30 minutes before slicing.
   - Slice the pastrami thinly against the grain for optimal tenderness.

8. Serve and Enjoy:
   - Serve the smoked pastrami on sandwiches with rye bread, mustard, and pickles, or enjoy it as part of a charcuterie platter.

Tips:

- The brining process is crucial for developing the classic pastrami flavor and texture. Make sure the brisket is fully submerged in the brine.
- Adjust the smoking time as needed based on the size of the brisket and your smoker's temperature.
- Store leftover smoked pastrami in the refrigerator and use it within a few days. It can also be frozen for longer storage.

Homemade smoked pastrami is a labor of love but well worth the effort for the incredible flavor and satisfaction of enjoying this classic deli meat at home. Enjoy your delicious smoked pastrami however you prefer!

Smoked Vegetable Skewers

Ingredients:

- Assorted vegetables of your choice, such as:
    - Cherry tomatoes
    - Bell peppers (red, yellow, green)
    - Zucchini
    - Yellow squash
    - Red onion
    - Mushrooms
    - Eggplant
    - Cherry or mini sweet peppers
- Olive oil
- Salt and pepper, to taste
- Optional: garlic powder, dried herbs (such as thyme or oregano)
- Wooden skewers, soaked in water for at least 30 minutes

Instructions:

1. Prepare the Vegetables:
    - Wash and prepare the vegetables by cutting them into bite-sized pieces. Ensure the pieces are similar in size for even cooking.
    - If using wooden skewers, soak them in water for at least 30 minutes to prevent them from burning during grilling.
2. Season the Vegetables:
    - In a large bowl, toss the prepared vegetables with olive oil, salt, pepper, and any optional seasonings like garlic powder or dried herbs. Coat the vegetables evenly with the seasoning mixture.
3. Skewer the Vegetables:
    - Thread the seasoned vegetables onto the soaked wooden skewers, alternating different vegetables for variety and color. Leave a little space between each piece for even cooking.
4. Preheat the Smoker:
    - Preheat your smoker to a temperature of about 225-250°F (107-121°C) using your preferred smoking wood chips or chunks (e.g., applewood, cherry, or hickory).
5. Smoke the Vegetable Skewers:
    - Place the assembled vegetable skewers directly on the smoker grate.

- Close the lid of the smoker and smoke the vegetable skewers for about 20-30 minutes, or until the vegetables are tender and lightly charred, turning them occasionally for even cooking.
6. Serve and Enjoy:
    - Remove the smoked vegetable skewers from the smoker.
    - Carefully slide the vegetables off the skewers onto a serving platter.
    - Serve the smoked vegetable skewers as a side dish or appetizer, garnished with fresh herbs if desired.

Tips:

- Customize the vegetable selection based on your preferences and seasonal availability. Try adding other vegetables like asparagus, broccoli florets, or Brussels sprouts.
- Experiment with different seasoning blends to enhance the flavor of the smoked vegetables.
- Serve smoked vegetable skewers alongside grilled meats, or as part of a vegetarian meal with couscous, rice, or salad.

Smoked vegetable skewers are a versatile and delicious dish that's perfect for summer barbecues, gatherings, or weeknight dinners. Enjoy the smoky goodness of these flavorful vegetables straight from the smoker!

www.ingramcontent.com/pod-product-compliance
Lightning Source LLC
LaVergne TN
LVHW081601060526
838201LV00054B/2010